Teaching Numeracy, Language, and Literacy with Blocks

Teaching

Numeracy, Language, and Literacy

with BLOCKS

Abigail Newburger and Elizabeth Vaughan

Redleaf Press
www.redleafpress.org

Published by Redleaf Press
a division of Resources for Child Caring
10 Yorkton Court
St. Paul, MN 55117
Visit us online at www.redleafpress.org.

First edition 2006
Cover designed by Amy Kirkpatrick
Interior typeset in Sabon and designed by Dorie McClelland
Interior illustrations by Chris Wold Dyrud
Interior photos by Elizabeth Vaughan, except pp. 41–42, photos by Brenda
  Pellow, and pp. 53–54, photos by Christine Beard
Printed in the United States of America
13 12 11 10 09 08 07 06   1 2 3 4 5 6 7 8

Redleaf Press books are available at a special discount when purchased in bulk for special premiums and sales promotions. For details, contact the sales manager at 800-423-8309.

Library of Congress Cataloging-in-Publication Data

Newburger, Abigail, 1932–
  Teaching numeracy, language, and literacy with blocks/Abigail Newburger and Elizabeth Vaughan.—1st ed.
    p. cm.
  ISBN-13: 978-1-929610-78-5 (alk. paper)
  ISBN-10: 1-929610-78-5 (alk. paper)
  1. Blocks (Toys) 2. Block building (Children's activity) 3. Educational games.
  I. Vaughan, Elizabeth. II. Title.

  LB1140.35.T68N49 2005
  372.133—dc22
                                        2005032026

Printed on acid-free paper.

To my two very special families, whose love and support through the years have made the adventure of life an exciting and joyous learning experience.

The first, my genetic family: The Newburgers, McLeods, Brewingtons, Olesons, Pragers, Moores, and Rothschilds.

The second, my Head Start family: Shippensburg Head Start, my other Head Start friends, and all the beautiful children.

—AN

To family, friends, and colleagues who continue to support me both personally and professionally.

To all early childhood professionals who work to support children and families.

—EV

Contents

Acknowledgments

Thanks to those people who reviewed early drafts of this manuscript and gave helpful advice, including Karen Ballard, Barb Bartels, Gail Gardner, Donna Keller, Judy Khan, Doris Kibler, Anne Nickles, Brenda Pellow, Karen Petty, Annette Searfoss, Toni Sherman, and Eileen Stecher; and to Christine Beard, June Clevenger, and Mabel Koser, who provided special support.

Thanks to Kevin Searfoss, whose computer knowledge and creativity were invaluable in the preparation of this manuscript, and to Bob Shirk, Jim Small, and Meg Newburger for understanding and valuing wood and its preservation.

Thanks to our very special young friends who modeled pictures for us: Anna Pettit, Grayson Pettit, Eileen Pomeroy, Megan Pomeroy, and Eric S. Reed.

Thanks to those programs that allowed us to visit and photograph their delightful children: Dickinson College Children's Center, Grace B. Luhrs Elementary School, Shippensburg Head Start, and Shippensburg University Child and Family Center.

And our especial thanks to Beth Wallace, our editor, for her wise guidance in pulling everything together to create the final work.

Introduction: How to Use This Book

This is a "how to" book. You do not have to read it through from beginning to end. The idea is to find the chapter that fits the child or children you are interested in, and then use the information in the chapter for working with them. The first three chapters lay a theoretical foundation for the rest of the book, with brief discussions of why blocks are used in the classroom (chapter 1), some rules on how children learn (chapter 2), and specifically how children learn language (chapter 3).

Chapters 4 through 10 each look at a different stage in block building. Here are some suggestions for using these chapters, which make up the heart of this book.

1. Start by looking at the **"Watch and Listen"** section. See if what you have seen and heard the child (or a group of children) doing fits the things listed. If so, that is the chapter for you to use.

   If not, try another chapter. The chapters cover stages from simplest to most advanced. If the child is two, look toward the beginning and move forward. If she is older, you may have to look at several chapters to find where she fits. The chapter titles may help you because they are descriptive of what you may be seeing the child do.

2. Next, look at the chart of things children learn at this level. This will help you know what to expect a child to learn through what he does and what you do with him.

3. After that, look at the list of materials to put in the block center to support that stage of learning. Start with a few things and add more as the child seems to lose interest in what is out.

4. Now look at the **"What to Do"** section. You will find that it usually tells you first to sit quietly by the child and watch and listen to what she is doing. This is a calming and personal way to introduce yourself to a child. Children usually love to have an adult sit down near them on the floor or on a small chair and just be there. It helps to build their self-image by implying "You are important. I want to be with you. You are worth my time." It also gives you time to see what the child is doing. What problem or question is the child trying to solve? You need to know this before you step in to take part in what is happening. You may see that the child needs something you can help her find. You may want to get something for her. For example, the child may be struggling with how to put one block across two

others to make a doorway shape. She is using a unit block and it keeps falling through, so you might quietly hand her a double unit and see what she does with it. Don't be surprised if she ignores your gift. She might be trying to figure out that she has to move the two uprights closer together. Your double unit doesn't solve the problem, but it was an idea. Sometimes it is better just to be there as moral support.

5. The next step is to look at the **"What to Say"** section. Try what it says. It suggests different ways to talk with the child. How you talk with the child depends on the child's language skills, which is also addressed in this section. Other examples of what to say are included in "What you might say to children in the block area" on page 33, which can be copied and posted in the block area as a reminder of the kinds of things to say to children as they are working with blocks.

6. Try to find time to make quick notes. Note how what you have done has worked for you and the children. Also note things you have learned about the child or the group. Occasionally take photos of the children playing in the block area. Then analyze the photos as we have done in the book. It is fun to see how many things you can discover about a child from a photo. You will get better and better at it. It will help you when making observational notes.

7. Read the **"What to Add"** part of the chapter. Decide what things you may want to add to the block corner. Decide how and when you will add them so they will help children grow.

8. Review the **"Watch and Listen"** section of the chapter and the chapter that follows it. When the child starts doing things that appear in the chapter that follows, move to that chapter and do the "What to" sections there.

Finally, chapter 11 covers some important safety issues concerning the use of blocks, and chapter 12 presents practical information on the care, selection, and types of blocks.

Now you are more than ready to get started. Have a wonderful time learning about all that children can get from blocks. It is a fresh and exciting way to inspire the joyous excitement of young, curious minds.

Why Blocks?

Why do we have blocks in the classroom? They are expensive. They take up lots of space. They have to be stored. It might seem as if they are more trouble than they are worth! But blocks are essential for children two to eight years old and beyond. Playing with blocks helps children develop important academic skills. Yes, blocks are worth the trouble! Here are some of the reasons:

- Children love to play with blocks.
- Children learn math, language, and science through playing with blocks.
- Children reach academic standards with the help of blocks.
- Children develop physically by using blocks.
- Children develop social skills in the block area.
- Children develop their creativity through block play.

Children love to play with blocks.

This has been true through the ages. If pieces of wood, cement, plastic, or even cake are available, children will build with them. Children can do whatever they want with blocks, and no one needs to tell them how to use them. The possibilities of blocks are open-ended. Children can play with blocks by themselves or with others. Blocks meet a special need that no other toy or learning material does.

Children learn math, language, and science through playing with blocks.

What children learn depends on their stage of development. For example, they learn about the complex concept of balance gradually, as they gain more experience with balance. They learn about it physically when they try to balance a long block (quadruple unit) on top of a tall unit (double unit). This also helps them to understand the scientific aspect of balance. Why and how does that quadruple unit stay on top of the double unit? They learn the mathematical aspect of balance when they make a symmetrical building. One side is equal to the other or the same as the other. This is basic algebra. They learn words connected with balance like *weight, size, same, lighter, heavier,* and so on. Because young children learn best by working with real materials, they can understand concepts like *half as much* or *twice as much* by seeing them demonstrated with blocks. The wooden blocks you see in most classrooms are designed to show this. They are based on a block called a *unit block.* All other blocks in the set have a math connection to the unit block. The half unit is a unit cut in half. It is also a square. The official names for the blocks teach words for math concepts—*double unit, quadruple unit, half unit.* They also help children see relationships. For example, two large triangles put together will make a rectangle. Children learn to estimate in their thinking—for example, they learn to figure out how many blocks will fit in a certain space.

Children reach academic standards with the help of blocks.

Blocks help children develop many skills that will help them to read and write when they get older. Many states have standards that tell us what preschool children should be able to do to succeed in grade school. Head Start also has national outcomes for what children should learn. The standards are often written in words that are hard to understand. They make you think that the only way to teach children is to sit them at tables and give them worksheets and tests. Some programs have to test children by law. Others have a choice. Even if you have to test them, remember that children learn by doing. Materials like blocks help them understand difficult information so they can take tests better.

Whether you have to test children or not, you can tell when they meet the standard by watching them play. You can also help children learn what is required by the standards through playing with them. Here are some examples:

1. You might see a standard that says something like this: "Sorts objects by one attribute." An *attribute* is a quality that an object has—for example, color, shape, and size are all *attributes* of materials. Children naturally see attributes like color, shape, and size. As they play with blocks, they naturally sort blocks by shape. When they build a tower, they want blocks that are the same shape. When they take part in cleanup, they learn to sort blocks onto matching outlines on the storage shelves (see chapter 12 for further details), and are thus learning to sort and match shapes. When they do any of these things, they are meeting the standard. They are sorting objects by one attribute: shape. If you keep track of which children are sorting blocks by shape, you know which children are meeting the standard. As you watch the children, you talk with them about how they are sorting units and half units. This way, you help them understand what they are doing. You help them have words to talk about what they are doing, and you help them to meet the standards.

2. Here's another example of a standard and how it can be taught through blocks. The standard says, "Begins to use language to compare numbers of objects with terms such as *more, less, greater than, fewer, equal to.*" As children build buildings, you talk with them about what they are doing. You can ask if they think John's tower has more blocks than Mary's. They wonder how to tell. You suggest a chart. Together, you count the blocks in John's tower. Then you mark off a square in the chart for each block. Next, you and the children do the same thing with Mary's tower, marking the blocks in the column next to John's. Now you all can see from the chart which one has more blocks. You have helped the children to use the language of counting to tell which is more. As you talk about the chart, the words *less than, greater than, fewer,* and *equal to* may also be used. When children begin to compare their towers to other children's buildings, they are meeting this standard.

The blocks can be a perfect way to help children think and learn. Often, a standard can give you a jumping-off place to help you teach what children need through play. This is better than sitting them down at tables because it is the way children learn best and most easily. You will find many examples of standards and how to use them playfully with your students in this book.

Children develop physically by using blocks.

Many classrooms do not have an indoor large-motor area. The block area becomes the place where children can develop coordination, strength, and flexibility. They are constantly using their legs and arms and bodies as they crawl, sit, jump up, walk, and lift. They carry heavy blocks from their shelves or bins and later put them back. They fill wooden trucks. They push them. They put blocks in buckets or boxes. They drag or carry them around. They fill their arms with them. They crawl from one end of a road to another with little cars. They add blocks here and there. They reach and stretch to place blocks where they want them. Their small bodies are in constant motion as they play with blocks. All of this builds and strengthens the muscles, bones, and ligaments of the children. In addition, children learn where their bodies are in space. They learn to judge where the blocks are in relation to other people and things so they don't hit or knock down other people or their buildings.

Children's small muscles are also busy with the blocks as they grasp the various shapes and sizes with their hands. Their fingers get better and better at controlling exactly where they want to put each block. They improve the way their eyes and hands work together as they carefully line up a tower of half-unit blocks. Children need this hand-eye coordination to read and to write.

Children develop social skills in the block area.

When playing with blocks, children have to work with challenging materials and other people. When they work together on building projects, children naturally develop social roles, like leaders and followers, workers and designers. They make up social rules that tell who will do what. A child who takes the leadership role tells others what to do: "Susie, get the double units and put them over there. José, you help her. Denota, you work on building the tower." When a child is a skilled leader, the others do what she says. They are agreeing to follow a social rule set up by the leader. There will be arguments among the children sometimes. When they work out the disagreements in a friendly way, they are growing socially.

Some young children may just be starting to be social. Even if they are not building with other children, they will learn social skills in the block area. They can stand and watch others play. They are learning from what they see and hear. A child can build alone. He can sit near another child. He can copy what the other child does. These are all ways that children learn.

A great deal of dramatic play takes place in the block center. Sometimes there is sharing between the dramatic play center and the block area. Children might make cars or planes for travel. They might make grocery stores, movie theaters, and furniture. In fact, putting the two centers side by side to encourage this pretend play is usually a good idea. This process opens all kinds of doors for the children's social growth.

Some children have trouble in the block area. They bump into people's towers. They step on and fall over people. They break what others are making. They refuse to follow the social rules set by the group. There are many reasons these issues arise. It is important to be aware of the children who are having difficulty moving carefully through the space, and to work to help these children develop their motor skills so they can better control their movements. It is also important to emphasize to others in the block area that these children are not doing these things on purpose; they are not intentionally being mean or hurtful.

When a child is purposefully destructive, she needs to be handled differently. This child may have chosen not to be part of the group. Your job will be to help her, in the best way possible, to learn how to be part of the group. It is important for you and others you work with to look for clues from children's behaviors that can help you understand why they are creating problems in the block area. The more you observe children, the more you will be able to see the subtle differences. Then you will think of ways to help them. When you can see the little clues, you will have a better idea of how to deal with the problem. You and other staff will have to plan carefully what you put out in the block center at different times and with different children.

Children develop their creativity through block play.

The block area is a wonderful place for children to create. At first, they explore the materials. In this book, the chapter on the Discovering period shows this. In the Towers and Roads period, the children continue to explore, but with more purpose. They decide to pile blocks on top of each other or lay them end-to-end. When they reach the Doorways and Bridges stage, we see a developing sense of beauty in the repeated arches they build. The Fences and Walls period brings out the drama in children. They start to use small figures in the enclosures. In the Patterns stage, the children's emerging sense of design and order flowers into magnificent structures built with care and great detail. Here they show an understanding of symmetry and visual balance. In the periods talked about in chapters 9 and 10, the children demonstrate that they have a very good understanding of blocks. They can now use them representationally to make whatever their imaginations desire. The Pretending period inspires the children's dramatic sense, and acting takes over. They plan, develop, and create all kinds of complex projects. The final period of Making Known Things extends what the children have done previously. In this period, the children visualize something they know. Then they plan and explore what is available to help them create what they have visualized. If they have a wide variety of blocks, older children and adults will create wonderful and beautiful things with blocks. Consider the continued popularity of Lego building blocks.

Because blocks are a high-interest play material and promote all areas of development and academic standards, they are an ideal material for use in the early childhood classroom. The purpose of this book is to show teachers of young children how this learning can be supported through observation and interaction in the block area. The focus on accountability and student achievement has pressured many teachers to use approaches that are inappropriate and ineffective with young children. We hope that by using this book, you will become more aware of the value of block play and recognize how your interactions with children support their learning.

Basic Learning Rules for Young Children

Young children learn the basics of language, literacy, and math through simple learning rules. These rules include the following:

- Young children learn by doing things, not just sitting and listening.
- Young children learn through all their senses.
- Young children learn best when something means a lot to them.
- Young children can *only* learn words they hear.

We will talk about the first three rules in this chapter. Because language is so important and affects all aspects of learning, we will talk about the fourth rule in chapter 3.

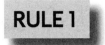

RULE 1

Young children learn by doing things, not just sitting and listening.

You may tell Johnny over and over, "Don't touch the heater. It will burn you." He still reaches toward it. If he touches it once and is burned, he won't touch it again. He may point to the heater and say, "No! Burn!" He has learned in one experience what all your words did not teach him. You can give children information by telling them something over and over. They will not understand or learn what you tell them. One reason for this is that they have very little word knowledge. Johnny has never experienced *burn,* so he doesn't know what you are talking about when you tell him the heater will burn. Before children can connect words to things, they have to have experiences with words connected to them.

When a child plays with water, he begins to learn about water. He feels that it is wet. He sees it, hears it, and feels it splash. He watches it flow from one place to another. He discovers it can be hot or cold. It fills and overflows. As you watch children play with water, notice the things they are learning about water and what they can do with it. Julio carefully fills a container until the water spills over. He is learning about overflowing. As long as he puts in more water than the container can hold, it will overflow. This is a law of science. If you talk about this with him, he will make a word connection to what he is experiencing. "Look, Julio, every time you put in too much water, it overflows. How do you do that?" If you told a child, "Sand is gritty," would he know what you were talking about? Not if he had never felt sand.

When children are doing what we call playing, they are learning about the things around them. They are learning what things do. They are learning what they can do with things. When a child uses a sieve with dry sand, he learns that the sand will go through. When the sand is wet, he has trouble making it go through. At this point you might ask, "The sand went through the sieve yesterday. I wonder why it doesn't go through today. What is different about the sand today?" You don't answer your own question. You ask the child to come up with an answer.

Children's logic is often fuzzy. A child may come up with a strange answer that you didn't expect. You don't correct the child, but try to get the child to think more. "That's a possible reason. Is there another you can think of?" You might help the child experiment. "You think it's because the sand is wet. Let's try an experiment. Here, start with some dry sand. Let's add just a little water. Let's try a tablespoon. Now mix that up. Does it go through the sieve as easily as when it was dry?" If it does, you suggest another tablespoon, and so on. Think of all the conversation that can happen as you and the child explore with water, sand, a sieve, and a tablespoon. The child is also learning to use and to name some tools (sieve and tablespoon).

When a child first starts to build a tower of blocks, it falls down. He discovers another science rule: If you build blocks high enough, they will fall down. Then he tries to build higher before they fall down. What are the things he tries? When you notice, you may point out to the child what he did. Do you think the child would learn the block-falling rule if he was told it and never played with blocks? Watch children. Tell them the blocks will always fall. They will still build over and over, testing the rule. Of course, they also like to see and hear and feel the blocks fall. It is fun!

Children love the building challenge. They love the power they have over the blocks. They can try to keep them up. They can also make them fall. Young children feel helpless a lot of the time. That is because they are small, and they don't yet know a lot. Also, they are just learning to use their bodies. Children often boast to cover up their feelings about not being able to do many things. When they can do things and control things, they feel good. When they learn to control the blocks and make them do what they want, they have ability and power over the blocks.

Can all these things mentioned above happen if a child is sitting and listening to someone telling him? No. Children cannot experience the blocks building up and falling down unless they build. They cannot feel strong and competent unless they build. These are all important parts of learning. Children learn naturally through working with materials. Their bodies have to try things. They can only watch and listen a *very* short time. They have to be doing. It is the way they are made and the way they learn.

To teach young children through play and experience, try these ideas:

- Add to classroom materials often.

- Take away things they no longer seem interested in.

- Give them lots of junk to play with. Be sure it is safe.

- Give them lots of paint, paper, glue, tape, markers, scissors, water, and other open-ended materials. What else can you think of that they like to work with?

- Let them make messes. Exploring with materials is often messy.

- Ask them to help you clean up when they are finished. They like to help. They will help if everyone is making the classroom neat and ready for what comes next. They will help if you and your fellow workers go about cleanup in a positive way. Cleaning up is a wonderful opportunity to teach things like classification and sorting, staying at a task, problem solving, and many other things.

◆ Let them play!

ACTION WORDS

These are some useful action words to use while children are playing. Remember that it is important for their learning to hear the words for what they are doing. We have left some blank spaces for you to put in your own action words as you think of them.

build	share	step
stack	teach	ride
pile	help	play
construct	turn	stand still
make	twist	wait
add	count	line up
create	talk	touch
lift	ask	pass
push	speak	keep
pull	write	save
roll	read	have
carry	observe	hide
hold	think	pretend
pick	listen	pantomime
balance	hear	kneel
place	see	_____
try	look	_____
find	fall	_____
enclose	tumble	_____
remove	crash	_____
sort	copy	_____
match	work	_____
transport	do	_____
move	plan	_____
empty	know	_____
fill	understand	_____
take	sit	_____
give	stand	_____

Young children learn through all their senses.

We noted in the last chapter that young children have to be "doing"; it's the way they are made and the way they learn. When we start to define *doing,* what do we think of? With young children, it means moving. The child has to move. He has to *go!* Where does he go? Usually toward something he sees that he wants to touch, to look at more closely, to smell, to listen to, or to taste. His senses are all there, pulling him to whatever interests him at the moment. He uses his senses to aid in the doing process of rule one. Without his senses, he could not learn through doing. Rules one and two go hand in hand. Doing with things is the way the child learns. In doing with things, the child uses, develops, and strengthens all of his senses. Give children things to look at and to feel, to hear and to taste, and, above all, to touch. Remember, sitting and listening only uses one sense. All the other wonderful ways to learn are being wasted when we ask children to sit and listen.

Here are some things you can do to help children learn through their senses:

- Give them things to see, hear, feel, taste, and smell.
- Cook with them. Use picture recipes.
- Be curious with them about things in nature. Use magnifiers and listen to nature sounds.
- Give them things to take apart and put together.
- Make rhythm instruments with them.
- Play with different things in water.
- Give them things to push, pull, empty, fill, and carry.
- Look at pictures with them.

SENSE WORDS

These are some useful sense words to use with children. Remember, the children need you to use the words so they can learn them! We have left some blank spaces for you to add your own sense words.

eyes	light	flashy
mouth	clear	loud
nose	opaque	distorted
ears	translucent	strange
fingers	vibrant	bang
toes	bright	crash
feel	dull	tiny
see	shimmery	huge
touch	shiny	zigzag
taste	sparkly	fuzzy
hear	warm	furry
red	cold	napped
blue	hot	bumpy
yellow	icy	wavy
green	hard	mushy
orange	soft	lumpy
purple	old	striped
black	new	icky
white	weak	sticky
brown	strong	soupy
pink	good	luscious
tan	bad	delicious
gray	smooth	velvety
peach	rough	vast
lavender	sweet	_____
shade	sour	_____
tint	yucky	_____
dark	salty	_____

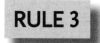

RULE 3

Young children learn best when something means a lot to them.

Let's think about memory for a minute. What things do you remember most? Are they happy, wonderful things? Are they sad, scary things? Are they important things that happened in your life? What people do you remember? Are they people who have meant a lot to you? These are the kinds of things most people remember. This is also true of young children. If we can connect the things we want children to learn to things that have important meanings for them, they will learn more easily. They will remember longer. Here is an example. Joey is playing with the blocks. He is talking about making rooms for the family. You might say, "I wonder how many rooms you will need." Then Joey and you might begin to list the family members. You put a block upright for each one. Then you count them and decide if Joey wants a room for each person. If he puts a person in each room, he is learning one-to-one correspondence, a very important math concept. If Joey decides to put Mom and the baby in one room, Auntie Sue and her daughter in a second room, and his brother and himself in another room, he is making sets of people. This is a simple beginning to set theory, which is another important math concept. Depending on how involved Joey is with his pretending, you might point out that his family is in three sets of two people. You might remark that that is interesting, three sets of two is six people. You must be careful not to get so excited about the concept you are teaching that you are talking away, but Joey isn't listening. You must learn to see when the child is no longer mentally involved.

Here are some important ways to learn about what is meaningful to a child:

- Ask the child's parents about his interests.

- Find out what the child likes and is interested in.

- Learn about the child's family, including animals and surrogate family members.

- Learn about the child's feelings. Is he usually happy? Does he frequently come to school in an angry mood? When is he fearful? How does he show his feelings?

- *Listen to the child.* We adults often start thinking about what we want to teach and forget to listen to children. What does the child talk about?

- Notice who the child plays with and how he interacts with others.

- Find out what books, toys, TV shows, and videos the child likes.

FEELINGS WORDS

These are some useful words to use when you talk about feelings. We have left some blank spaces for you to add words of your own.

happy	concerned	well
super	fearful	tired
jolly	helpless	unfriendly
joyful	hesitant	_____
gleeful	hurt	_____
laughing	lonely	_____
smiley	troubled	_____
warm	worried	_____
witty	angry	_____
comfortable	furious	_____
excited	grumpy	
friendly	mad	
funny	ornery	
great	frustrated	
mellow	jealous	
mild	pouty	
open	sorry	
quiet	sad	
thoughtful	reluctant	
willing	crazy	
capable	wild	
close	surprised	
afraid	embarrassed	
scared	humble	
anxious	hopeful	
apprehensive	sick	

Talking about Math

We take a lot for granted when we use math terms with children. For example, we assume children understand that the numeral 5 represents five things, such as five blocks. Some children have a lot of trouble understanding that one symbol, "5," can be the same as five things (✳ ✳ ✳ ✳ ✳). It doesn't make sense to them. That is why we count objects, we count on number lines, and we have puzzles with the numeral and the number of objects. Blocks are ideal for counting. Children love the challenge, "I wonder if you can make your tower one block higher." They also need to learn the connection between cardinal numbers (for example, *one, two, three*) and ordinal numbers (for example, *first, second, third*): "The double unit is first in the line. The half unit is second. If you put your unit block right there, it will be the third. Let's count them: One, two, three. First, second, third."

Words that describe position in space are important. Blocks can be on top, under, next to, beside, near, ahead, behind, and with. Opposites are found in block building: tall/short, wide/narrow, big/little. Size, shape, and amount are also there. These are words found in geometry and algebra.

You will find a section on what children learn about math in each of the Stages of Block Play chapters.

MATH WORDS

Here is a list of math and building words that will help develop mathematical thinking. We have given you some space at the end to add your own words. We have not thought of them all.

large	high	twelve
small	low	thirteen
full	whole	fourteen
empty	half	fifteen
first	all	sixteen
second	none	seventeen
third	nothing	eighteen
fourth	everything	nineteen
fifth	light	twenty
over	heavy	next
under	up	many
around	down	few
through	out	some
beside	in	greater than
above	forward	less than
between	backward	plus
below	wide	minus
behind	narrow	last
front	tall	add
middle	short	subtract
back	count	circle
more	one	square
less	two	triangle
a lot	three	rectangle
little	four	bottom
big	five	top
same	six	_____
different	seven	_____
equal	eight	_____
single	nine	_____
double	ten	_____
triple	eleven	_____

Basic Learning Rules for Young Children— Language and Literacy

In the last chapter, we talked about the first three of the four learning rules for young children. Here are the four learning rules again:

- Young children learn by doing things, not just sitting and listening.
- Young children learn through all their senses.
- Young children learn best when something means a lot to them.
- Young children can *only* learn words they hear.

In this chapter, we are going to talk about the fourth rule and how children learn language. This is very important to children's learning, because everything else they learn is communicated through language. If they have a lot of words and are comfortable using them, they do much better in school.

Young children can *only* learn words they hear.

The way children learn language is amazing. It is a difficult process. As you read, think about this process. Think about how you might put it to use as you work with children who have little or no language.

This is how it works: As babies are *spoken to,* they pick up the sounds that are used in their language. They store them in their minds. They try to say the sounds. They practice them as they babble. Their babbling begins to sound more and more like the language they hear. When an adult plays and talks with a baby, she names people (mommy), things (bottle), and actions (go). The baby begins to connect meaning to the words she hears. She starts to copy the words she hears. She starts to say words in connection to things, people, and actions. In the beginning, some sounds are hard for the baby to say. This is because her mouth, tongue, and lips are just strengthening and learning to work together. She becomes more understandable with practice and development. The more words the adult gives to the child that are connected to things, people, and actions she can see or experience, the more she will learn. Children who are blind connect words to things they hear, feel, smell, taste, or experience. Children who are deaf connect signs used by adults to things they see, feel, smell, taste, or experience.

How Babies Learn Language

The baby sits alone with the ball. She pictures the ball in her mind. She does not know what it is called.

An adult comes and plays ball with the baby. She calls the ball a "ball" as they play. The baby now has in her mind the picture of the ball and the word "ball." She may try to say the word "ball."

The adult plays with the baby with three balls of the same size. She calls them "balls." The baby now sees in her mind three balls and adds the word "balls" to her word collection.

Next, the adult comes with a smaller ball. She calls it a "ball." The baby is uncomfortable, because her mind picture of balls shows them all the same size. After a while, she adds the ball to her ball picture, because it's called a "ball." Her ball picture now allows balls of different sizes.

Finally, the adult comes again to play with the child, this time with an orange. She shows the baby the orange. The baby looks at the orange and says, "Ball." The adult says, "No, it's an orange." The baby is even more uncomfortable than when she added the smaller ball to her mind picture. That was a ball. Now she has to change her mind picture again. Not all round things are balls. Some round things are oranges. She makes a new mind picture with two groups. She sees a group called "balls" and then another group called "oranges."

As adults play with children and name things for them, children develop more and more mind pictures with words attached to them. If they didn't have the names attached to them, they would be like the baby alone at the beginning. They could see the mind picture, but they wouldn't be able to talk about what they saw. They wouldn't be able to ask for it. They couldn't get it if someone asked them to. They wouldn't be able to read about it—all because they didn't have the word to go with their mind picture.

The more words a child has, the better she will be able to talk with people. The more words she has, the better she will understand what people say to her. When she learns to read, she will be taught to sound out words. If she sounds out a word she has never used before, she might be able to say the word. However, the word will have no meaning in the sentence she is trying to read. That is why it is so very important for adults to constantly name things for the children they work with. That way, the children will have more and more words in their minds.

This is also why talking with children is so important. When you talk with children, you have a chance to add words to their vocabulary. For example, a child may comment, "Me and John played ball." You might respond by asking, "That's very interesting. Which ball did you play with?" Then the child would have to think of a way to tell you which ball it was. She might say, "The big white one." In order to build her language, you might add, "Oh, I know, the big white one with red spots on it. Is that right?"

Conversation is a give-and-take between people. When you ask questions that make children come up with thoughtful answers, the conversation is able to continue. You do not necessarily know what answer the child will give. When you ask a question that can have only one answer, and you know the answer you want the child to give, it's a closed question. It stops conversation. Once the answer is given, there is nothing more to say. For example, you ask a child, "What color is this block?" The child says, "Red." Then you ask, "What color is this one?" The child may answer "blue," or she may not answer at all. Children quickly tire of this kind of questioning. It really is testing them. Even at a very young age, children learn to dislike being tested. It is not a give-and-take between people; it is one-sided. When you ask closed questions, you make the child who has to come up with an answer uncomfortable. When a person is uncomfortable, she doesn't want to converse.

In the same situation, you can ask a child, "What could you build with these red blocks?" This is an open-ended question. There is no right answer. The child will have to come up with the words to describe something in her head. This is an advanced language skill. This kind of question can lead to a conversation with a child. You can talk about her building for a long time. The longer you talk with her, the more she is learning.

Here are some ways you can help children learn language:

- Talk with them.

- Say the names of things.

- Talk about things they do.

- Describe things. For example, say, "See the round red ball roll."

- Read many books the children enjoy.

- Sing songs and say rhymes with the children.

- Use the same words over and over.

Let's talk for a minute about the child who is learning two languages at the same time—her native language at home and English at school. Do you remember all the things the child learning one language has to think about? Imagine what it is like for the child trying to learn two languages! This child has to have two words in her mind for each thing. She also has to understand how both languages work. They probably do not work exactly the same way. For example, in German the action word is put at the end of the sentence, while in English it is in the middle.

You will often notice that a child who is learning two languages is completely silent in the classroom. This is because she is listening and learning. She will look at you with wide eyes and refuse to say anything. This can become frustrating because you are sure she understands what you are saying to her. This may be true. Second-language learners usually understand what is said to them before they are able to speak the language. Be gentle with them and accept that they are not yet ready to try to speak. They will eventually try a few English words along with their native language. In time, they will start to make whole English sentences. This is the developmental process, and it takes time and much patience.

For this process to take place, it is important to make children feel comfortable in the classroom. Think about how you can make children feel at home in the classroom. Try to add things from all the children's cultures. Remember how important things that mean a lot are to a child's learning. Find out what kind of blocks children play with in her country. There might be some with letters from her alphabet that you could add. The Spanish alphabet, though similar to the English alphabet, has variations. Native flags might be fun to use with blocks for decorating buildings. Ask the children's parents for help.

Here is another thing to think about when you try to teach the beginning letters of words. In English, *tree* begins with T, while the Spanish word for tree *(árbol)* begins with A. Sometimes when you ask a child who is learning Spanish at home and English at school what the word *tree* begins with, he will say, "A." Is he wrong? These are important things to think about. Be aware of them as you work with your second-language learners. Like all your children, they are beginning learners, and they have even more to learn than the others. Understand this. Take care to speak more clearly for them. Think about how truly difficult it is for them and be endlessly patient. When they have learned both languages, they will have a huge advantage as adults. Think about all the children who learn only one language as preschoolers and then spend years studying another language in high school. It is important to support children who are learning two languages as preschoolers to help them be truly bilingual.

We cannot leave a discussion of words without addressing words that are important to the subject of literacy. Early childhood programs are being asked to teach literacy. One necessary part of literacy understanding is the use of words related to books. The following is a list of those kinds of words.

WORDS FOR BOOKS AND READING

Here are some important words you will want to give children so they will be able to talk about books and reading. We have left some blanks so you will be able to add words as you think of them. We haven't thought of them all.

book	when	events
page	where	sequence
word	why	retell
letter	how	_____
sentence	poem	_____
syllable	verse	_____
phrase	quotation	_____
front	story	_____
back	play	_____
top	title	_____
bottom	author	_____
left	illustrator	
right	fact	
spine	reality	
punctuation	nonfiction	
period	opinion	
comma	fantasy	
question mark	fiction	
exclamation mark	beginning	
capital	middle	
uppercase	end	
lowercase	before	
print	after	
writing	alphabet	
reading	subject	
who	character	
what	setting	

Literacy Development

What do children learn about literacy through blocks? The charts on the following pages will show you. We have related children's literacy development to typical early childhood learning standards. This will help you show how block play helps children meet standards.

READING CHART

What the Child Does	Reading Standard/Outcome	What You Can Do
Reads familiar signs, such as "Stop"	•Recognizes environmental print, including logos and signs	Provide road-sign props and familiar store and business signs.
Asks the teacher to read something to her	•Demonstrates an understanding that illustrations and print convey meaning	Provide labels, signs, and related books. For example, place books about cars and trucks with transportation toys.
Reads familiar words	•Recognizes a word as a unit of print, that letters are grouped to form words that form sentences, and that words are separated by spaces	Provide labels, signs, and related print materials. Label the block center and the block patterns on shelves.
Identifies capital letters or punctuation	•Recognizes some conventions of print (e.g., capital letter, period, question mark)	Use writing conventions in charts and signs (capitals, periods, question marks, etc.). Chart example: "How many blocks did we use in our building?" Sign example: "Bob's house."
Looks at written materials in the center	•Demonstrates an understanding that different forms of text have different purposes	Provide related written materials, such as train schedules, tickets, signs, and train books.
Looks at books or other print material	•Develops book handling skills	Provide books and magazines with pictures and information related to block building, such as bridges, roads, and skyscrapers.
Points to and names familiar letters	•Recognizes letters of the alphabet	Provide alphabet books about buildings and construction. Use letters in chart labels (list A, list B, list C).
Uses the first letter of a word to guess what it is	•Shows progress in associating the names of letters with their shapes and sounds	Make letters out of blocks. Talk about the shapes of blocks compared to the shapes of letters.
Reads new, unfamiliar words	■Uses knowledge of phonics, word analysis, syllabication, picture and context clues to decode and understand new words	Introduce new vocabulary related to block activity. When building a boat, label its parts, such as *hull, stern, starboard.*
Looks at books; uses the Internet to find pictures of buildings	■Locates information using appropriate sources and strategies	Provide books; encourage use of the computer to look up information

•Quoted from the Pennsylvania Early Learning Standards
■Quoted from the Pennsylvania Academic Standards

WRITING CHART

What the Child Does	Writing Standard/Outcome	What You Can Do
Writes horizontal lines of scribble	•Uses scribbles to communicate in writing	Provide writing utensils and small strips of paper to make signs for buildings.
Draws pictures	•Uses recognizable drawings to express thoughts, feelings, and ideas	Provide drawing materials; encourage the child to draw her building. Sit in the block area and draw children's buildings. Post drawings or photos of children's buildings in the block area.
Writes a string of letters and symbols	•Uses letterlike forms, letters, or random letter strings to express thoughts, feelings, and ideas	Provide writing materials for the child to write about her building. Have her make a sign naming her building. Make a second label with the word written correctly and post it next to the child's sign.
Writes her name	•Writes own name and other meaningful words	Provide label-making materials and a sign-up sheet for taking turns in the block center.
Asks how to write a word	•Explores letter-sound associations while writing	Encourage the child to write what she hears; pronounce words slowly for her.
Tells the teacher about her building	•Begins to represent experiences through pictures, writing, dictation, and play	Write what she says about her building and post it near her building.
Looks at written signs in the block area	•Understands that writing serves a variety of purposes	Provide a variety of written labels, signs, labeled maps, and directional charts. By labeling where materials are to be stored on the shelf, you can help the child use the signs to clean up materials.
Writes sentences describing her building	▪Writes informational pieces using illustrations when relevant	Encourage the child to write about how she constructed her building. Help her draw diagrams or pictures to illustrate what she has written.
Writes a description using correct capitalization, punctuation, and spelling	▪Edits writing using the conventions of language	Have the child read her description. Point out where she used capital letters or punctuation such as periods or question marks.

•Quoted from the Pennsylvania Early Learning Standards
▪Quoted from the Pennsylvania Academic Standards

RELATED SKILL DEVELOPMENT

What the Child Does	Fine-Motor Standard/ Outcome	How This Supports Literacy
Picks up blocks with fingers	▲Demonstrates control, strength, and dexterity to manipulate objects	Fingers are strengthened for holding and using a pencil.
Places the blocks where she wants them	▲Demonstrates hand-eye coordination	Hand-eye coordination is necessary for controlling letter formation and placing letters in a line.
Aligns the blocks as he builds	▲Demonstrates ability to use writing, drawing, and art tools	Increasing control results in improved pencil grip.

▲Quoted from the Head Start Child Outcomes Framework

What you might say to children in the block area

Describe what the child is doing or has done. Here are some examples:

"You filled the truck."

"You made a tower."

"You made a line of blocks."

"You laid them end-to-end."

"You made a corner here."

"You made a place for your animals."

"You used symmetry. You have the same blocks on this side as on the other."

"You have made four corners. Did you notice that?"

"You have made a pattern —a red cube, then a

yellow, then a red, then a yellow."

"I notice you have put a row of triangles across the top of your building. It makes a pretty decoration."

Here are some examples for the child with little language:

"Truck's full."

"A tower."

"A tall one."

"Long block."

"Row of blocks."

"Line of blocks, one, two, three."

"A triangle."

"You slide the block."

"Blocks together make noise."

"Hard."

"Hold the block."

"Pick it up."

"Put it down."

"Put it in."

"Take it out."

Use the names of the blocks to help the children recognize them. Here are some examples:

"That's a unit block."

"Can you hand me that long, quadruple unit?"

"You put two small trian-

gles together. You made a half unit. You're right—a half unit is a square. How did you know that?"

"That's a ramp you're sliding your car down."

"Want to try a Gothic arch to make two roads?"

Ask "how" and "wonder" questions. Here are some examples:

"How did you make that tall tower?"

"I wonder what will happen if you add another block?"

"I wonder how many blocks are in it?"

"How could you make the road come over to Susie's house, here?"

"I wonder if something lives inside your fence?"

"You have made four corners. I wonder why you did that?"

"I wonder which color cube will go next in your pattern?"

"Would you like to tell me about your building?"

"Would you like me to write the story of your building?"

Add your own ideas

_____   _____   _____

_____   _____   _____

Discovering

This beginning stage of block play usually starts with toddlers. This is the stage in life when young children explore and find out very simple things about the materials they work with. They pick up blocks and feel all their sides and corners. They put them in their mouths. They put them in containers and pour them out. They drag them around. They do not actually do much building with them yet. Older children who have never played with blocks before may go through this stage, but very quickly.

Start with these materials in the block corner.

Store the blocks in dishpans or drawers with photos of the contents on their sides and inside bottoms.

- A small set of wooden unit blocks: 24 half units, 24 units, 24 pillars, 10 half columns, and 16 small triangles

- A collection of plastic buckets, baskets, bins, and other interesting containers the children can fill and empty, push and pull, and carry about

- Small collections of blocklike objects of foam or other soft materials

Watch and Listen

Does the child

- look at and feel a single block?
- lift a block above his head, rub it on the floor, throw it, pick it up, and put it down?
- bang a block against things?
- carry blocks around the room?
- put blocks into things and take them out?
- put blocks in his mouth?

What to Do

If the child is doing a number of the things in "Watch and Listen," you can

- sit quietly by the child. Watch what he is doing.
- follow the child's lead. Do some of the things you see the child doing.
- talk about the blocks he has.
- talk about what he is doing with the blocks.
- do things with the blocks yourself. Do some of the things listed in "Watch and Listen."
- build a tower or a road. Notice if the child starts to copy you. If he does, move to chapter 5.

Don't ask the child to name shapes or colors. Say them to him.

What to Say

If the child speaks with only one or two words, use short sentences like these:

"A block."

"A square block."

"Smooth."

"It feels smooth."

"It's smooth."

"Hard."

"Hard block."

"It's hard."

"It feels hard."

"Slide."

"Slide it."

"You slide the block."

"Lift bucket."

"Heavy."

"Bucket is heavy."

"Carry the bucket."

"You push."

"You are pushing the blocks."

"Round."

"It's round."

"Go round and round."

If the child uses lots of words and talks naturally, use sentences like these:

"Wow, that's a big block you have."

"You can lift it high in the air."

"You put a lot of blocks in the bucket."

"It makes a bang when you hit it against the floor."

"That's a different sound."

"It makes a different sound when you hit the bucket."

If the child talks to you, respond naturally to what she says. Your objective is to help the child understand in words what she has learned from her play with blocks. You want to help her thinking develop.

Use the names of blocks or shapes or colors as you talk. (See the unit block chart in chapter 12 for names.)

"You filled the pan with unit blocks."

"You like the feel of the small triangle."

"That half column is round."

"Look at all those squares you have."

"Round and round the edge."

"You are feeling around the edge."

"That is a circle shape."

"Your bucket is full of unit blocks."

What to Add

As the children get used to the blocks you have out, remove some of the things the children seem tired of.

If the children are filling and emptying, here are some things you could add:

- cardboard boxes to fill with blocks and push around.
- different sizes and shapes of buckets, baskets, and bins. Even include little baskets that will hold only one or two blocks.
- a few large wooden or plastic trucks or trains. Do not use tin trucks that have sharp metal edges. Children can be cut on them easily.

If the children show more interest in the blocks themselves than in what they do with them, here are some things you could add:

- a set of small wooden blocks in primary colors. Sometimes they come in a wooden wagon.
- a set of cube-shaped alphabet blocks.
- other sets of small blocks with different shapes.

Think about what you see the children doing. What will help them develop more? Add to what you say when you add things. For example, the colored blocks give you a chance to talk about colors. "Oh, look, you have a little red unit block."

What Are Children Learning in the Discovery Period?

MATH		
What the Child Does	**A Sample Learning Standard**	**Notes**
Empties and fills any kind of container available	•Develops concepts of space and shape	A very young child begins to discover that a container holds only a certain amount. For example, when her bucket is full, Tashana stops trying to put in more blocks.
Feels sides, corners, and thicknesses of blocks	•Develops concepts of space and shape	A very young child learns about *angles, length, width, thickness,* and *shape.* She does not know what they are called. She knows what they look and feel like. She also learns about surfaces, like *round, flat,* and *curved.* She begins to make connections between similar objects in her thinking. For example, Latrina spends a lot of time picking up and feeling different blocks against her cheek and putting them in her mouth.
Lifts or carries blocks or containers of them	•Develops and uses measurement concepts	A very young child begins to feel weight and balance within herself. She is beginning to understand what weight is and to compare different weights. Barbara walks around with two similar buckets filled with blocks. She has one in each hand. She seems to be balancing them.

•Quoted from the Pennsylvania Early Learning Standards

What Are Children Learning in the Discovery Period?

TALKING AND LISTENING

What the Child Does	A Sample Learning Standard	Notes
Fills containers with blocks. Pushes, pulls, carries, and empties the containers as the adult talks about what he is doing.	▲Understands an increasingly complex and varied vocabulary	The child begins to understand words like *push, pull, fill, empty, throw,* and *carry.* For example, when an adult asks Hugo to empty his bucket of blocks into the box, he will do it.
Plays with different kinds of unit blocks. An adult gives him the names for the blocks he is playing with.	▲Understands an increasingly complex and varied vocabulary	The child begins to understand words like *block, unit, triangle, square,* and *wood.* For example, Mike gives the teacher a unit block when she asks for one.
Starts to use some words like *big* and *full* that have to do with math as he plays with blocks. A nearby adult adds words as he plays with them.	▲Uses an increasingly complex and varied spoken vocabulary	The child begins to understand and use math words like *empty, full, little, big, a lot,* and *same.* For example, Damian might say, "Got lots a (of) blocks."
Begins to say some color words when given colored blocks to play with. An adult talks about the colors of the blocks.	▲Uses an increasingly complex and varied spoken vocabulary	The child begins to understand and use words like *red, blue,* and *green.* He also will understand other descriptive words when an adult uses them. For example, an adult seeing Robin rubbing his hand across a smooth board might say, "Smooth, smooth, smooth," and the child might then say, "Smooth," too.

▲Quoted from the Head Start Child Outcomes Framework

What might this little boy be doing?

Your thoughts:

_____

_____

_____

_____

You might say to him:

_____

_____

_____

_____

If he has little language, you might say to him:

_____

_____

_____

_____

What might this little boy be doing?

Our thoughts:

1. He seems to have put a lot of blocks in the truck.
2. He is now emptying all the blocks out of the truck.
3. He knows how to empty them. He can turn over the truck.
4. He is working alone.
5. He has stayed at the task for quite a while.
6. It looks as though he has only used *unit* blocks. Did he sort them out? Were they just the closest ones? You may want to watch this in the future.

This little boy may be starting to learn to match the blocks to the shelf pattern. Normally, we would see this in the next developmental period. In this period, we would have bins or baskets with pictures because the children are less able to do the hand-eye work of fitting the blocks to the patterns.

Notice the patterns of the blocks on the shelf.

You might say to him:

"You *filled* that truck so *full*."

"Now you are *emptying* it."

"You *turned over* the truck."

"The truck is *heavy*."

"It is hard to *empty* the truck."

"You used *unit* blocks. They look like this." (Show him the block.)

"You are *pushing* the truck *over*."

If he has little language, you might say:

"Truck *full*."

"You *empty*."

"*Big* truck."

"*Lots of* blocks."

"*Heavy*."

"You *work*."

"*Push!*" (Say as he pushes over the truck.)

What might this little boy be doing?

Your thoughts:

_____

_____

_____

_____

You might say to him:

_____

_____

_____

_____

If he has little language, you might say to him:

_____

_____

_____

_____

What might this little boy be doing?

Our thoughts:

1. He seems to have pulled out a lot of blocks.
2. He is cradling the only wooden block among them in his arms. We wonder if he likes the properties of wood better than foam.
3. Notice how his fingers are around the edge of the block. Is he feeling the edges? Does he notice the sharpness of the edge? Is he feeling the smoothness of the wood?

Notice the block pattern on the front of the shelf. It has the name of the kind of block that goes there printed on the block. Notice that the longest edge is parallel to the edge of the shelf. This suggests the direction the blocks should be placed on the shelf. The reason for this is that when the blocks are all shelved, you can see which size block is there. If they were shelved with the end sticking out, you wouldn't be able to tell.

You might say to him:

"You're holding a *long* block."

"It is called a *double unit* block."

"It's *smooth*."

"You're *feeling* the *edge*."

"That's an *edge*." (Point to the edge.)

"It has *a lot* of *edges*. See?" (Point to the edges.)

"Your block is *made of wood*."

"It is *hard*. It is *heavy*."

"I think it is *fun* to *hold* blocks."

"I think they are *comfortable* because they are so *smooth*."

If he has little language,

you might say:

"*Long* block."

"You *hold* block."

"*Smooth* block."

"*Lots of* blocks." (Point to the pile.)

"*Heavy*."

"*Hard*."

"*You feel*."

Towers and Roads

In the Towers and Roads period, children pile blocks on top of other blocks. They become very good at this. They like to build as high as they can. Some children carefully place blocks so they are perfectly aligned on top of others. Some children will move them around with their fingers until they are even. They have discovered that this helps the towers go higher. Children also line up blocks all over the floor. When they run into a wall and can no longer build straight, they have difficulty deciding what to do. They do not understand how to make corners yet. They often copy others' buildings. They frequently talk to themselves or to others. They share blocks and take a role in a building project. One child does the building while another hands her the blocks. A child who is just beginning to be comfortable with blocks and people might work beside another child. They don't interact. This is called *parallel play*. Children in the Towers and Roads period may stay there a long time. They will continue to build towers and roads but will add things to them that show they are developmentally beyond the period.

Start with these materials in the block corner.

Store the blocks on shelves marked with photos or tracings of each kind of unit block. Names of the blocks should be printed in lowercase letters on the patterns or on the photos.

- A set of wooden unit blocks. See the "Number of Unit Blocks to Have" chart on page 130 to find out how many you should have. Notice what a large number of blocks you should have. Classrooms rarely have enough blocks. At this stage, the unit blocks are all you really need. The children's objective is to build high or wide. They especially need lots of units and half units for building high. Adding double units helps to extend their roads.

- A space where the children have room to spread out their blocks. Ideally, it should be a space where the buildings can be left up until the children are ready to take them down.

- Hard hats to protect the children from falling blocks. Hard hats that you can buy for dramatic play work well. Have as many hats available as the number of children who can play in the block corner at one time.

- A flat, hard-surfaced rug can be included so that the noise of falling blocks is muffled.

Watch and Listen

Does the child

- pile blocks one on top of the other?
- line up the blocks end-to-end?
- carefully place the blocks and manipulate them with her fingers so they are in perfect alignment?
- copy the structures of others?
- talk to herself or with others?
- share blocks and take a role in working with other children (one child is the builder, another hands blocks to her)?
- work next to a child without interacting?

What to Do

If the child is doing a number of the things in "Watch and Listen," you can

- sit quietly and watch what the child is doing. (Support the child by being there.)
- respond naturally to what the child is saying if she talks. Encourage conversation. Talk with the child about what she is doing. (Do this only if it won't disturb the child's concentration.) Talk about the materials she is using.
- build with blocks yourself, making careful towers or roads. (This may give the child ideas.)
- try making towers with a base made of several blocks. (This might help the child get an idea how to make her tower stronger.)
- share blocks yourself. (If a child needs one of your blocks, give her one. Divide the blocks you have in equal piles and give her one of the piles.)
- ask open-ended questions that allow the child to answer any way she likes. Ask questions for which you don't have an answer. Only ask questions if they won't disturb the child's concentration.

Don't ask the child to name things. These are testing types of questions, and they make children uncomfortable. This kind of questioning stops conversation that builds language.

What to Say

If the child speaks with only one or two words, use short sentences like these (see page 33 for more ideas):

"You pile."

"You pile blocks."

"You are piling blocks."

"Tall."

"High."

"A block tower."

"A high tower."

"Look! A tower."

"It balances."

"Looks like a road."

"A long road."

"You build."

"You made a road."

If the child uses lots of words, talk naturally. Use sentences like these:

"You've made a tall tower." "Your tower is really high." "One, two, three, four, five, six, seven, eight, nine, ten. Wow, it is ten blocks high."

"You are working so carefully. You put one block at a time and straighten it before you put another. That way you will be able to build higher."

"You have made a long road. It is twelve blocks long."

Use the names of blocks or shapes as you talk. (See the unit block chart in chapter 12 for names.)

"You made a road with units here, and then you added double units here." "I notice you are building with double units. They are longer than units. You can make a road with fewer blocks."

"You are building that tower with half units. They are square."

As you share blocks, you could say, "I have a floor board like that one. Do you need another? Here, you may have mine."

"I notice you are using small triangles. Here, may I hand them to you as you work?"

Ask open-ended questions that allow the child to answer any way he likes.

"How did you get it so high?"

"How did you make it balance like that?"

"I wonder what would happen if you added this block."

"Would you like to tell me about your tower?"

"I wonder why you put this block here. Did you have a special reason?"

"I'm curious. How did you make that corner there?"

What to Add

As the children get used to what you have out, add some of the things in the following list and remove some of the things the children seem tired of.

- Think about what you see the children doing. What will help them develop further?
- Add to what you say when you add things. For example, as you add a *crossroad* block, you might ask children who are building roads, "I wonder if you could use this. Do you have any ideas about what you could do with it?"
- Have a digital camera for taking pictures of the children's creations and use them in books or on walls of the center.
- Put pictures of towers and roads on the walls of the center for the children to copy. They can be actual photos of things or photos of block buildings you can find on the Internet.

If the children are building towers,

- add *pillars* and *columns* of various sizes. When you add them, talk about them with the same kind of question as mentioned above. You might also use them in building a tower to help the children get some ideas.
- add *floor* and *roof boards* to give a better surface for building, if you have a rug in the center.
- add a set of alphabet blocks. They are great for building towers, and they might encourage some letter-naming conversations.

If the children are building roads,

- add unit blocks that help roads to become more interesting and that challenge the builders, like *half circle curves, Gothic arches, right angles, side roads,* and *ramps.* Use the same kind of question as mentioned above.
- add things to the center as the children seem to need them. When children talk about cars, add cars. If they want trucks, add them. You can add many kinds of vehicles as time goes by.

What Are Children Learning in the Towers and Roads Period?

MATH		

What the Child Does	A Sample Learning Standard	Notes
Counts blocks in a tower with help from an adult	•Uses counting and numbers as part of play	At this stage, when the child starts to count things like the blocks in a tower, he points to a block and says, "One," then to the next and says, "Two," and so on. He is connecting a number to an object. This is called one-to-one correspondence.
Takes down a tower one block at a time with adult help	▲Progresses in ability to put together and take apart shapes	Mostly, children want to knock down a tower. If an adult can get a child to take the tower down one block at a time, he will experience a reverse operation. This is like subtraction, but with real things. This is very difficult for young children.
Says or shows by actions the building is going to fall	•Makes predictions based on observations and information	The child shows he can predict cause and effect. A child may say, "If I add another block, it will fall," or, "It's going to fall!"
Builds matching towers or roads next to one someone has already built	•Recognizes how things are alike (comparisons)	The child makes comparisons between his and another's building. He may think this to himself or talk about it. He begins to understand equity and inequity. Joe says, "Jose's tower is taller."

•Quoted from the Pennsylvania Early Learning Standards
▲Quoted from the Head Start Child Outcomes Framework

What Are Children Learning in the Towers and Roads Period?

TALKING AND LISTENING

What the Child Does	A Sample Learning Standard	Notes
Counts the blocks in a block tower with help from an adult	▲Begins to associate number concepts, vocabulary, quantities, and written numerals in meaningful ways	The child begins to understand and use counting words like *one, two, three*. She begins to understand that the last counting word tells "how many." For example, Tara says as she counts blocks, "One, two, three. I have three."
Talks about where a block is	▲Builds an increasing understanding of directionality, order, positions of objects, and words such as *up, down, over, under, top, bottom, inside, outside, in front of,* and *behind*	The child begins to understand and use words like those in the standard. In addition, she understands and uses *balance, align, predict, unstable, equal, unequal,* and *same* when adults use them while talking with her. For example, Laurie remarks to Diane, "Put that block on top."
Talks about what she is doing as she builds	▲Uses an increasingly complex and varied spoken vocabulary	The child begins to understand and use words like *stack, pile, lay, move,* and *turn*. For example, Isha says to Amanda as she is putting a block on her tower, "Turn it. Turn it. Yes, like that."
Names unit blocks as she puts the blocks away	▲Uses an increasingly complex and varied spoken vocabulary	The child uses the names for the unit blocks. She begins to use words for what she has built, like *row, line, tower, road*. For example, Sara says to Caitlynn as they clean up, "Get the squares. I'll get the units."

▲Quoted from the Head Start Child Outcomes Framework

What might this little boy be doing?

Your thoughts:

_____

_____

_____

_____

You might say to him:

_____

_____

_____

_____

If he has little language, you might say to him:

_____

_____

_____

_____

What might this little boy be doing?

Our thoughts:

1. He has piled ten blocks on top of each other.
2. He places them with care, watching what he is doing.
3. He appears to be concentrating very hard.
4. He is working alone.
5. All of the blocks he is using are the same (unit blocks). We wonder if he had a variety to choose from and chose the one kind.
6. The boy is using his right hand and pincer grasp.

Notice that the blocks are foam unit blocks. They come in different colors. They have very different physical properties from wood blocks. Some programs use them because they don't hurt as much when someone is hit with them. They have a very different feel. They tend to stick to each other and not slide, as wood ones do. They are much lighter. They have square corners. When they are chewed, teeth marks are left. They are cheaper. They are squeezable. They do not have the satiny smoothness of wood. They have a somewhat rough texture.

You might say to him:

"Look, you have made a tower."

"I wonder how you built that tower."

"I wonder how tall a tower you can build."

"It is really fun to build up with blocks."

"I wonder if you can take down the tower without it falling. That is really hard. I bet you can do it."

"I think there are at least ten blocks in your tower. How could we find out?"

If he has little language, you might say:

"You *pile*."

"You *pile* blocks."

"*One* on another."

"Look! A tower."

"You made a tower."

"*Tall*. A *tall* tower."

"*Higher, higher*." (Say as he piles each block.)

What might these children be doing?

Your thoughts:

_____

_____

_____

_____

You might say to them:

_____

_____

_____

_____

If they have little language, you might say to them:

_____

_____

_____

_____

What might these children be doing?

Our thoughts:

1. They have made a short road and have lined up two baby tigers and two baby lions on the road tail to tail.
2. The blocks are not evenly lined up. This may be partly because foam blocks don't slide, so they are hard to align.
3. The children seem to be interacting.
4. They seem to be actively involved in what they are doing.
5. They seem to have sorted the adult and baby wild animals from a number of cows.

We would probably watch and listen for a while to try to find out what they are playing.

Though children in this stage usually are more interested in the building, these children seem to be very interested in the wild cats. We can almost see them playing *The Lion King.* Even though they have built a road, they may really be in a more advanced stage of block development. We would want to follow their block building for several days to see what else they did.

You might say to them:

"I notice you've built a little road."

"Your animals seem to be having a parade. I wonder where they are going."

"Your road has three different colors: blue, green, red. I wonder how you decided to make it that way."

"You have two baby tigers and two baby lions in your parade. I wonder how many that is all together."

If they have little language, you might say:

"Block road."

"Five blocks: one, two, three, four, five." (Point to them as you count.)

"Wild animals. Tigers and lions."

"Colored blocks. Blue block. Green block. Red block. Three colors."

Doorways and Bridges

During the Towers and Roads period, children do their building with the widest side of the blocks. In this period, they discover that blocks can be balanced on end. They learn to balance double and quadruple units on their narrow end. They may spend hours trying to put a unit block across two upright units, and it will fall through over and over. Finally, they discover that they need to move the two upright blocks closer together. They also find that using a longer block will work. You can tell children these truths or show them. Usually, you will find that they have to prove it to themselves by trial and error. When children are ready, they learn it fairly quickly. Once they have the concept, they may build doorways on top of each other to make a tower with windows. They may also build two tall towers on a doorway base. They will build one bridge after another, making what looks like a raised highway. They will do many variations on these themes as they build. As with the previous period, the children will talk to themselves. They will share blocks and work together on a building. Some children will still play next to one another but not interact (parallel play).

Start with these materials in the block corner.

Store the blocks on shelves marked with photos or tracings of each kind of unit block. (Refer to chapter 5 for a list of essential items that should be in the block corner in every developmental period.) Names of blocks should be printed in lowercase letters on the patterns or on the photos.

- A set of wooden unit blocks. See the "Number of Unit Blocks to Have" chart on page 130 to find out how many you should have. It is more important to have the number of blocks recommended than to have a wide variety of different kinds of blocks. When you have a large number of unit blocks, the children can really explore their possibilities. In the last period, you started with a few kinds of unit blocks. You will have added a number of kinds as the children have increased their exploration. By now there will be *double* and *quadruple units* on the shelf. There will also be *pillars* and *columns* of different lengths. The *Roman arch* is a useful block for this period.

- Plastic containers or bins with the following items:
  - plastic, rubber, or wooden cars, trucks, and boats.
  - plastic, rubber, or wooden people (families with different skin colors and community helpers of different races and genders).
  - plastic, rubber, or wooden animals (farm, forest, jungle, sea, and so on).

Watch and Listen

Does the child

- begin to place blocks on end in upright positions?
- try to put a block across two uprights without success?
- find a block that fits across?
- repeat an operation over and over once he's learned it?
- build upward with one doorway on top of another?
- talk to himself?
- share blocks and take a role in working with other children? (One child is the builder, another hands blocks to the first. One child may be the leader in telling children what to do, or the children will naturally take on roles.)
- work next to another child without interacting?

What to Do

If the child is doing a number of the things in "Watch and Listen," you can

- sit quietly and watch what the child is doing. (Support the child by being there.)
- ask yourself these questions: Is he busy? Is he trying different things with the blocks?
- decide if he seems to be learning about the blocks. Does he need you to do anything?
- talk with the child about what he is doing. (Do this only if it won't disturb the child's concentration. If the child is busy building, he probably won't hear you.)
- write down what the child tells you about his construction (with his permission). It can be copied and put in his portfolio, and a copy can be taken home.
- make notes about what you see happening. What exactly is the child doing? Who is the child involved with? How is he involved?
- build bridges or doorways yourself to use as models.
- avoid telling the child how to build a bridge. He will need to discover this for himself by trial and error.
- take a photo when he has discovered how to bridge with a block. Let him take it home.

What to Say

Talk about what you see. If the child speaks with only one or two words, use short sentences like

"Block's on end."   "You bridged."   "Looks like a
"It balances."   bridge."

If the child uses lots of words, talk naturally. You might say

"Look how you can balance those double units on end."

"You put four double units in a row."

"There's a double unit between each one."

"You put a double unit on top of those two blocks. How did you do
    that?"

"It looks like a bridge."

"It looks like an elevated highway."

If the child talks about a bridge or a door, say something like

"I wonder where the door goes" or "I wonder what is under the
    bridge."

"Would you like some boats to use with your bridge?"

Ask open-ended questions.

"How did you do that?" "How did you make that block stay up?"

If she says it's a bridge, you might have some boats in the center the
    next day and say, "You made a bridge yesterday. I thought you might
    like some boats to go under a bridge if you build one today."

"How did you make those blocks stay up on the supports?"

What to Add

As the children get used to what you have out, add some of the things you kept back and remove some of the things the children seem tired of.

- Think about what you see the children doing. What will help them develop further?

- Add to what you say when you add things. For example, as you add pieces of construction paper cut to look like a pond, you might ask children who are building bridges, "I wonder if you could use these. Do you have any ideas about what you could do with them?"

- Have a digital camera for taking pictures of the children's creations and use them in books or on walls of the center.

- Put pictures of doorways and bridges on the walls of the center for the children to copy. They can be actual photos of things or photos of block buildings you can find on the Internet. Find pictures of doorways that are made with *post and lintel* construction: two uprights with a beam across the top. (Barns have doors like this.) Label the pictures with simple words.

- If children are making doorways, add the *Gothic arch* and *door*. This is a different kind of doorway for the children to explore. At this stage, children start to find uses for *large triangles*.

- After listening to their conversation, add vehicles, people, or animals that might fit their play. If these are already out in bins, put the bins in a prominent place and say, "You wanted some cars to go through your doors yesterday. I got them out for you."

If children are making bridges,

- add construction paper cut in the shape of ponds and rivers. These can be laminated for more permanent use if the children use them often.

- after listening to the children, add things that fit their needs. If they have used your construction-paper water, you might add boats of different kinds and put out ramps prominently.

- add *floor* and *roof boards* and pieces of heavy cardboard.

These children may be developmentally ready to use sign-in sheets. They may also start to make signs to protect their buildings. Put out pieces of card stock, tape, markers, and tongue depressors for this. Let children write using any script they are comfortable with (scribbles are fine!).

What Are Children Learning in the Doorways and Bridges Period?

MATH		
What the Child Does	**A Sample Learning Standard**	**Notes**
Tries over and over to make a block bridge a space between two blocks	▲Builds an increasing understanding of directionality, order, and positions of objects	The child develops an understanding of width (a visual understanding of what will fit across a distance). He also learns an important architectural form called *post and lintel*.
Moves cars or animals under a built bridge	•Demonstrates awareness of measurement attributes (length, volume, weight, area, time, and temperature)	The child develops an understanding of what will fit *between* and *under*. He is learning about *width* and *height*.
Makes one bridge after another to create what looks like a raised roadway	•Shows an awareness of symmetry	The child makes structures that look the same on both sides. He is showing a beginning understanding of *symmetry*. This indicates he is developing an understanding of visual balance. When he creates the same construction over and over, such as when he makes one bridge after another, he is showing an inner sense of patterning.
Figures out how to solve a structural problem with his building	•Uses simple strategies to problem solve	The child begins to understand how supports work. He uses them to improve the balance of his building. For example, Domingo puts a second unit block inside his doorway. He says, "It's to make it stronger."

•Quoted from the Pennsylvania Early Learning Standards
▲Quoted from the Head Start Child Outcomes Framework

What Are Children Learning in the Doorways and Bridges Period?

TALKING AND LISTENING		
What the Child Does	**A Sample Learning Standard**	**Notes**
Talks about how she drove cars *through* the tunnel	▲Builds an increasing understanding of directionality, order, positions of objects, and words such as *up, down, over, under, top, bottom, inside, outside, in front,* and *behind*	The child continues to add words that are useful in talking about math concepts, like *over/ under, through, estimate,* and *to bridge.* This happens when there is a lot of conversation between the child and adults. For example, Angela says, "I'm putting this [block] over the other blocks."
Names the different parts of what she is building	▲Develops increasing abilities to understand and use language to communicate information, experiences, ideas, feelings, opinions, needs, and questions; and for other varied purposes	The child begins to understand and use words connected with building doorways and bridges, like *floor, roof, bridge,* and *doorway.* For example, Leticia says, "Look at my *doorway.* I made a doorway!"
Talks with other children as she builds	▲Grows in recognizing and solving problems through active exploration, including trial and error, and interactions and discussions with peers and adults	The child uses questions and answers in working with others. She explains what she means. For example, Gabriel asks Brenda, "What should we use to make that bridge longer?"

▲Quoted from the Head Start Child Outcomes Framework

What might this little girl be doing?

Your thoughts:

_____

_____

_____

_____

You might say to her:

_____

_____

_____

_____

If she has little language, you might say to her:

_____

_____

_____

_____

What might this little girl be doing?

Our thoughts:

1. She has put a *number* of *double units* on *end in a row*.
2. She has *bridged* them with *double units*.
3. She has repeated the process *five times*.
4. She is *putting* the ends of two blocks *on the top of* one block. This is difficult to do. Earlier in the period, a child would put two *uprights* near each other and *place* each block on one upright end.
5. She appears to be really *concentrating*.

You might say to her:

"Look at how you have *balanced* those blocks *on top* of the other blocks. I bet that was hard. I wonder how you did it."

"It is interesting that you have used *only double units* in your *construction*. Did you have a reason to do that?"

"You have *made five* bridge *shapes* that look the *same*. Did you notice that? It *makes a pattern*."

If she has little language, you might say:

"Blocks *balancing*." (Point to the ones on top.)

"*One, two, three, four, five. Five* blocks."

"*Lots of* blocks."

"Blocks *standing up*."

"Blocks *on top*."

What might this little boy be doing?

Your thoughts:

_____

_____

_____

_____

You might say to him:

_____

_____

_____

_____

If he has little language, you might say to him:

_____

_____

_____

_____

What might this little boy be doing?

Our thoughts:

We wonder what you are thinking about this picture. This boy has made several very nice enclosures. Enclosures come in the next period, Fences and Walls. But he is trying to make the block bridge the space. This is why it is so important to watch and listen to children. That is how we learn about them. Let's look at what we see here.

1. The boy understands how to make enclosures.

2. He is still struggling with the problems of corners. Notice that at his end of the building, he has the blocks on either end of the end unit block. If this doesn't make sense, get out some unit blocks and try it. At the end closest to us, he has put the end unit blocks against the ends of the side units. Until he understands corners, he may not be able to understand why his block falls through.

3. He still seems to be struggling with the problem of bridging. He even seems to have the idea of moving the support blocks in. See how he has pushed the sides toward the center. Really, he seems to understand bridging, but what he understands doesn't work because he doesn't understand cornering yet. You might want to build a copy of his building next to his and explore it with him with "I wonder" questions.

You might say to him:

"You seem to be having a problem with that block. It won't *go across very well*, will it? I wonder why that is. What did you do to *make it work?* I wonder if you could change the building some way so it would work. Let's look at the *corners.* How did you make them? Did you make them the *same* at *both ends?*" (This kind of questioning will help him figure out the solution.)

If he has little language, you might say:

"Block *falls through.* Wonder why. Can we *fix?* Look at *corners.*" (Point to the differences.) "*See.* Not the *same.*"

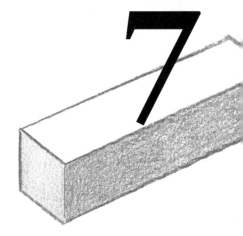

Fences and Walls

In previous periods, the children explored the widths and ends of the blocks. In this period, they are interested in the edges of the blocks. They put them on their sides end-to-end to make long walls. It is in this period that they finally figure out the corner. They make corners easily now and are able to make walled spaces, like fences, rooms, cages, and so on. Sometimes they have a lot of trouble when they try to make an enclosure. This is because they connect the end of one block to another differently. This makes the square end up crooked. Here we see some true beginnings of dramatic play. Until now, the building has been the thing they are interested in. Now, they make farms with animals in fences. They begin to talk about making houses and garages. They put people in rooms and cars in garages. They also start to place the blocks on top of each other on edge. They make doors by placing a unit on end and making it swing in and out. As with previous periods, they still copy one another's buildings. They talk to themselves and with others. They share blocks and take roles in working cooperatively with other children. Some still continue parallel play.

Start with these materials in the block corner.

Store the blocks on shelves marked with photos or tracings of each kind of unit block. (Refer to chapter 5 for a list of essential items that should be in the block corner in every developmental period.) Names of the blocks should be printed in lowercase letters on the patterns or on the photos.

- A set of wooden unit blocks. See the "Number of Unit Blocks to Have" chart on page 130 to find out how many you should have. It is more important to have the number of blocks recommended than to have a wide variety of different kinds of blocks. When you have a large number of unit blocks, the children can really explore their possibilities. Add the *half Gothic arch* and the *small buttress* to the large collection the children now have to work with. When children have enough blocks and enough space to spread them out, they are more likely to make real, serious constructions and less likely to misuse them.
- Plastic containers or bins with the following items:
  - plastic, rubber, or wooden cars, trucks, and boats.
  - plastic, rubber, or wooden people (families of different races and community helpers of different races and genders).
  - plastic, rubber, or wooden animals (farm, forest, jungle, sea, and so on).

Watch and Listen

Does the child

- place blocks on their sides end-to-end?

- place blocks so that they make corners and fences?

- put the blocks on top of each other on edge?

- make doors in fences and garages?

- talk about making a fence, a farm, a zoo, a house, or another thing that is an enclosure?

- talk to herself or others?

- share blocks and take a role in working with other children (one child is the builder, another hands blocks to the first)? One child may be the leader, or the children will naturally take on roles.

- work next to a child without interacting?

What to Do

If the child is doing a number of the things in "Watch and Listen," you can

- sit quietly and watch what the child is doing. (Support the child by being there.)

- ask yourself these questions: Is she busy? Is she trying different things with the blocks?

- decide if she seems to be learning about the blocks. Does she need you to do anything?

- talk with the child about what she is doing. (Do this only if it won't disturb the child's concentration.)

- write down what the child tells you about her construction (with her permission). It can be copied and put in her portfolio, and a copy can be sent home. Ask if she would like that.

- make notes about what you see happening. Who is the child involved with? How is she involved?

- add different props or plastic figures depending on what the child is talking about. (If the child doesn't refer to pretend things—farm, house, garage, and so on—don't add things.)

- build enclosures yourself to give models. Add a second layer of blocks to the wall, for example.

What to Say

If the child has little language, you might say

"A wall."

"A long wall."

"Look, a corner."

"Round the corner."

"Horse in fence."

"Mom's beside fence."

"You over there."

Talk about what you see. You might say

"I notice you put three blocks in a straight line."

"You made a corner and put two blocks in a line."

"You made four corners. Did you notice that?" "You made an enclosure." "It's like a pen."

If the child talks about a farm, zoo, house, garage, or other enclosure, say something like

"I wonder what animals live in your zoo."

"Would you like some animals to put in your zoo?"

Ask open-ended questions.

"I'm really curious about your construction (or what you have built). Would you tell me about it?" If the child says it's a garage, you might have the bin of cars out in the block center the next day and say, "You made a garage yesterday. I thought you might like some cars today. Maybe you can make a garage for them."

"How did you make that corner?"

Talk about the work.

"You have really worked hard to build this."

"You have spent a lot of time and work to make your house."

"You must be tired after all the work you have done on your farm."

Respond naturally to what she says to you. Encourage conversation.

What to Add

As the children get used to what you have out, add some of the things you kept back and remove some of the things the children seem tired of.

- Think about what you see the children doing. What will help them develop further?

- Add to what you say when you add things. For example, as you give them the bin of farm animals, remind them that they were talking about a farm yesterday. "I thought you might like to add to your farm today. Could you use some of these animals on your farm?"

- Have a digital camera for taking pictures of the children's creations. Use them in books or on the walls of the center.

- Put pictures of fences and walls on the walls of the center for the children to look at. They can be actual photos of things or photos of block buildings you can find on the Internet. Add photos of constructions made by the children. Be sure the children have enough blocks to work with.

- Add props and small figures that fit what the children say they are building. For example, add farm animals and people for the farm; zoo animals, trees, paper ponds, and rocks for the zoo; and dollhouse furniture for a house.

- Put a prop box in the block area that fits what the children say they are building. For example, add a mechanic's box for the garage builder.

- Add sign-making materials for labeling their buildings: markers, tape, scissors, index cards, tongue blades, and so on. (Remember that whatever they write is okay—from scribbling to words.)

- Add a flip-book of words and pictures connected with what the children have been building (farm, zoo, garage, house, and so on).

- Add some of the rainbow blocks with colored plastic windows in them or water or bead blocks.

- Add figures with disabilities.

What Are Children Learning in the Fences and Walls Period?

MATH		
What the Child Does	**A Sample Learning Standard**	**Notes**
In the Discovery period, the child felt angles. In Towers and Roads, he made angles sometimes by accident. In this period, he makes corners on purpose in order to construct rooms and pens.	•Recognizes, names, describes, builds, draws, and compares two- and three-dimensional shapes	The child makes corners using two blocks at right angles to each other. For example, Yazil takes four double units and puts them together in a square shape. He comments, "I made a square."
Uses blocks as doors in walls	•Determines whether or not two shapes are the same size and shape	The child puts doors in house walls and swings them in and out very carefully. He has some understanding, through trial and error, of which size and shape of block to use to fit the opening in the wall. He does not have a perfect understanding. For example, Matt places three double units so they make three sides of an enclosure. He then makes the last side of the enclosure with three units. They stick out beyond the ends. That doesn't seem to matter. The central unit becomes the door.

•Quoted from the Pennsylvania Early Learning Standards

What Are Children Learning in the Fences and Walls Period?

TALKING AND LISTENING

What the Child Does	A Sample Learning Standard	Notes
Uses words to compare amounts she has with what others have	▲Begins to use language to compare numbers of objects with terms such as *more, less, greater than, fewer, equal to*	The child begins to understand and use math words like those in the standard. For example, Jade says as she compares the number of blocks she has to the number Makayla has, "You have fewer blocks than I do. I can give you three. Then we will be equal."
Uses more naming words when talking about the blocks she builds with	▲Progresses in clarity of pronunciation and toward speaking in sentences of increasing length and grammatical complexity	The child begins to understand and use words like *corner, fence, wall, enclosure,* and *place.* For example, Kristy says, "I'm making a corner here in my wall."
Talks with other children as she builds	▲Progresses in ability to initiate and respond appropriately in conversation and discussions with peers and adults	The child gets involved in serious discussions with peers. She gives long explanations in great detail. She exchanges ideas with other children. For example, Destiny says to Mabel, "Your fence is running into my fence because that block is too long, and it is going this way, and you can move it that way, and it will be okay."
Names what she is building	▲Develops growing abilities to plan, work independently, and demonstrate care and persistence in a variety of art projects	The child begins to think about what she is doing and makes plans. Judy says as she is making a pen shape, "I am making a sty for this big fat pig."

▲Quoted from the Head Start Child Outcomes Framework

What might this little girl be doing?

Your thoughts:

_____

_____

_____

_____

You might say to her:

_____

_____

_____

_____

If she has little language, you might say to her:

_____

_____

_____

_____

What might this little girl be doing?

Our thoughts:

1. This little girl has made three fenced-in areas.
2. Into each one she has sorted a large farm animal and a small one (mother and baby, perhaps).
3. She appears to have rejected the dinosaurs behind her on the floor, or perhaps they are wild animals and don't belong in pens.
4. She has used *half units* and *half pillars* to construct them. We wonder if she ran out of *half units* or had another reason. The lying-down cows are in the pen made of the lower blocks. The pen toward the back has one low block at the back of the cow. The pens share a side with a large block and another pen. Was this because of a limit in the number of blocks?
5. She has laid the blocks at the corners so the length of each wall is different. This is a common problem in this period. You can see how she turned the block in to solve it.

We have a number of questions we might like to ask. If we knew the classroom, we would know if there were enough of the *half units*. This might make us think about buying more if we had the budget. It would be very interesting to see how the child would respond when we asked if she ran out of blocks. We have tried not to name the spaces she has made to see if she will tell us what they are.

You might say to her:

"Tell me about what you are making. I see two farm animals in each space."

"I see a *big* and a *little* animal."

"You have put a *set* of *two* in each space."

"I wonder *how many* animals are in all the spaces put together."

"So we might say that *three sets* of *two* make *six* altogether."

"I notice you used *half units* for the horse and this cow (pointing) and *half pillars* for the cow that's *lying down*. Can you tell me about that?"

If she has little language, you might say:

"*Three* spaces." (Point at the spaces.)

"*Two* horses. *Two* cows. *Two more* cows."

"*More* cows. *Fewer* horses."

"*Big* and *little* animals."

What might this little boy be doing?

Your thoughts:

_____

_____

_____

_____

You might say to him:

_____

_____

_____

_____

If he has little language, you might say to him:

_____

_____

_____

_____

What might this little boy be doing?

Our thoughts:

1. This little boy is making a walled box.
2. He is using the skill learned in the previous period with blocks on end. We wonder if he also builds with the blocks on edge. (See chapter 6.) We may want to watch for this the next time we observe him in blocks.
3. He has solved the problem of the corners that the previous little girl was still working on. He had the same problem in the picture in chapter 6.
4. He appears to be right-handed.
5. He is balancing the blocks on end to build up a second row of blocks.
6. He is using wooden blocks. Did he have a choice of foam blocks?
7. He is looking away from what he is doing. His concentration has been broken for a moment.

This is a problem for those of us watching children. Is it better just to watch, or should we join in, in some way? This is a judgment call. You are the only one who can decide at that moment in time.

You might say to him:

"It looks like you're building a *high* wall. I wonder if you are planning to *keep something inside it.*"

"You've built with *unit* blocks today."

"You made a *floor* for your box. Nothing will be able to *get out under* the wall."

"It's an interesting building. Your walls are *made* with the blocks on *end.*"

If he has little language, you might say:

"A *box.*"

"You *made* a *box.*"

"*Unit* blocks."

"*Using unit* blocks."

"*Corners.*" "*See* the *corners.*" (Point to them.)

Patterns

At last, the children have learned what they need to know about what blocks can do. Now they put all they know together and truly start to create buildings that have a sense of beauty. As they build, they seem to feel an inner need for order, and they work to make the buildings the same on both sides *(symmetrical)*. They put a block on one side and then a like block in a similar place on the other side. They also feel the need to decorate what they build. They use small triangles and blocks, beads, bottle caps, and more to put patterns on their works of art. They use all they have learned about the properties of blocks to build buildings that have complex windows and arches and doorways. They have porches supported by columns. They build structures with different heights and thicknesses of columns that are symmetrical. They continue to talk to themselves and others. They work together to create buildings. At this stage, they may also prefer to create by themselves.

Start with these materials in the block corner.

Store the blocks on shelves marked with photos or tracings of each kind of unit block. (Refer to chapter 5 for a list of essential items that should be in the block corner in every developmental period.) Names of the blocks should be printed in lowercase letters on the patterns or on the photos.

- A set of wooden unit blocks. See the "Number of Unit Blocks to Have" chart on page 130 to find out how many you should have. It is more important to have the number of blocks recommended than to have a wide variety of different kinds of blocks. When you have a large number of unit blocks, the children can really explore their possibilities. Add the *small triangle, small half circles* and *quarter circles* to the large collection the children now have to work with. When children have enough blocks and enough space to spread them out, they are more likely to make real, serious constructions and less likely to misuse them.

- Bins of different kinds of small things for decorating buildings

- One-inch colored cubes

- Bottle lids—from many from kinds of bottles, in different colors

- Parquetry blocks

Watch and Listen

Does the child

- begin to make buildings that are the same on both sides?

- make more complex buildings that have sides, windows, and arches?

- put decorations on the building that form a pattern? For example, does he use small triangles and blocks in a pattern across an arched structure?

- seem to make a pattern with the blocks just for the pattern itself, without any structure in mind?

- work with other children in making patterns and buildings with decorations?

What to Do

If the child is doing a number of the things in "Watch and Listen," you can

- sit quietly and watch what the child is doing. (Support the child by being there.)

- ask yourself these questions: Does he seem to be planning the pattern? Does the pattern just seem to happen? Does he talk about what he is doing?

- make notes about what you see happening. What blocks does he place first, second, and so forth? Does he try a block somewhere, remove it, and put it somewhere else?

- talk with the child about what you see him doing.

- talk about the kinds of blocks the child is using.

- play with blocks yourself and make patterns.

- listen and respond to his comments naturally, if the child talks about his construction. Encourage conversation.

What to Say

If the child has little language, you might say

"A pattern. Red, blue, red, blue, red, blue. A pattern." (Point to the parts of the pattern.)

"A pillar here. A pillar here." (Point to like items on each side of the building.)

"A pillar." (Point to one.)

"A pillar." (Point to the other.)

Talk about what you see. Say things like

"Did you notice how you have put a row of small triangles across the top of your building? It makes a pretty decoration."

"Look, you've made a pattern. See, a triangle here, then a square, then a triangle, then a square. That is a pattern."

"You used symmetry in your building. Look, you have put the same things on both sides." (Tell what is alike on each side as you point them out.)

"I really like the pattern you made with your blocks. May I copy it?"

"It is interesting the way you made a pattern with red and yellow cubes. A red cube, a yellow cube, a red cube, a yellow cube."

"Oh, I see, a big block, a little block, a big block, a little block. You are making a pattern. Did you notice that?"

"It is interesting the way you made a pattern with red and yellow cubes. May I copy it?"

Ask open-ended questions.

"I notice that everything you put on this side is the same as everything you put on that side. How did you do that?"

"I see you have made a pattern. Can you tell me how you made it? I wonder how you will decide what to put next?"

Use the block names in talking about them.

"A unit, a double unit, a unit, a double unit, a unit. I see a pattern here."

"Wow, you used pillars and columns and made a pattern with them."

What to Add

As the children get used to what you have out, add some of the things you kept back and remove some of the things the children seem tired of.

- Think about what you see the children doing. What will help them develop further?

- Add to what you say when you add things. For example, as you give the children a bin of large, clear-colored beads, say, "You were making really nice patterns on your buildings yesterday. Here are some beads I thought you might like to use."

- Have a digital camera for taking pictures of the children's work. Use the pictures in books or on the walls of the center at the children's eye level.

- Be sure the children have enough blocks to work with.

- Add a set of colored blocks. Sometimes they come in a wagon. Provide a storage place for them, like the wagon they came in.

- Add a set of foam blocks, so the children can experience a different material with different properties.

- Have some pattern cards. (Do not make the child use them, but point out when he makes one of the patterns naturally. You can also compare a pattern the child has made to one of the cards. Use them yourself so the children can see how it is done.)

- Have photos of buildings that show patterns or symmetry on the wall.

- Have books that show pictures of different kinds of symmetry or pattern.

- Add shells, beads, pebbles.

- Add three or four sets of blocks with different architectural elements, such as roofs and turrets. Sets can be found with names like *architectural blocks, Arabian blocks, Oriental blocks, Baroque blocks,* etc.

What Are Children Learning in the Patterns Period?

MATH		
What the Child Does	**A Sample Learning Standard**	**Notes**
Decorates her buildings with patterns in blocks	•Sorts, categorizes, classifies, and orders objects by one attribute	The child is sorting, classifying, and ordering objects when she puts them in a pattern like red, blue, green, red, blue, green. For example, Destiny puts a line of colored cubes in a pattern across the front of her building.
Notices patterns others have made and begins to copy them	•Recognizes, describes, and extends patterns	The child understands that a pattern can be copied. She can use pattern cards. The child will use and become good at using pattern cards after she has shown the ability to make patterns somewhere else, as in blocks.
Sorts objects by size and color in decorating a building	•Sorts, categorizes, classifies, and orders objects by more than one attribute	The child will be able to sort by color and shape, not just by color. She will sort from a pile of different-colored objects all the red circles and the blue triangles.
Begins to build structures that are symmetrical	•Shows an awareness of symmetry	The child understands that things can be balanced by weight. She now also sees how a building can look balanced (the same on both sides). For example, Crystal carefully places an upright unit block on one side of a Gothic door. Then she puts one just like it on the other side. She will place similar pieces one at a time on each side until she has made a symmetrical building.
Makes long blocks balance on top of tall blocks by putting similar things on each side of the center point	•Develops an awareness of seriation. Compares attributes such as length (shorter/taller), size (bigger/smaller), and weight (heavier/lighter) in everyday situations.	The child understands how the balance used in weighing works. If one side goes down, she adds weight to the other side.

•Quoted from the Pennsylvania Early Learning Standards

What Are Children Learning in the Patterns Period?

TALKING AND LISTENING		
What the Child Does	**A Sample Learning Standard**	**Notes**
Talks about large triangles and a rectangle as he plays with blocks	•Recognizes geometric shapes in books, artwork, and the environment	The child shows an understanding of different shapes. He can use the names of them in conversation. He can make one shape out of two others. For example, Jamari says, "Ms. Smith, look! I made a square with two small triangles."
Talks about how one building is different from another building	•Demonstrates awareness of measurement attributes (length, volume, weight, area, time, and temperature)	The child begins to understand and use words like *measure, close together, far apart, closer, farther away, wide, narrow, like, different,* and *compare.* For example, Dakota says to Mike, "Look at all the triangles Hans used in his building. Sam used pillars and columns. They are really different."
Talks about the patterns he has put on his buildings when asked about them by an adult	•Explains why and how objects are organized	The child uses and understands words like *arch, column, pillar, symmetry, pattern, castle, temple, fort, mansion, construction, building, design, alike, repetition, copying,* and *crenellation* (a serrated or wavy edge) when an adult has used them in conversation about blocks. For example, Austin tells his teacher, "My castle has tall towers made of columns. See the design I put here on the front." He can give an explanation to an adult.
Starts to tell stories with plot about the buildings he is building	•Responds and makes connections to story events and characters by relating personal experiences	The child is beginning to tell stories through dramatic play with blocks. For example, Raja excitedly tells Ms. Palmer, "My fort has a giant ogre. He is going to eat up all the ladies of the village."

•Quoted from the Pennsylvania Early Learning Standards

What might this little girl be doing?

Your thoughts:

_____

_____

_____

_____

You might say to her:

_____

_____

_____

_____

If she has little language, you might say to her:

_____

_____

_____

_____

What might this little girl be doing?

Our thoughts:

1. She is making a *symmetrical pattern*.
2. She seems to have just put the *half circle* needed for the *pattern* on the *arch*.
3. She appears to be right-handed.
4. She seems to be really concentrating on what she is doing.

Notice how the *pattern* moves out from a central *single* block. She is using a complicated *design* with a *number* of *different* types of blocks. This program has an *extra small* block set that the girl is using *on top* of the *units*. See how the variety helps her *creativity*. Notice how she has used a *double unit* and two *unit* blocks to make a *quadruple unit* for her building base. You might want to note the different types of blocks she is using. We wonder what she would do with a box of plastic lids to choose from.

It would be interesting to ask her about her *construction*. If she is really *concentrating*, you may want to watch and listen to find out more about it.

You might say to her:

"I am interested in your building. Would you like to tell me about it?"

"I see *symmetry* in your building. See how you have made it to look *the same* on each side. That is called *symmetry*."

"How did you make it look that way?"

"You solved the problem when you didn't have enough *quadruple* blocks. You used *one double unit* and *two unit* blocks."

If she has little language, you might say:

(Point to the blocks.) "The same. That's symmetry."

"What do you think?"

"*Half circles. Rectangles. Arches.*"

"*Lots of different shapes.*"

What might this little girl be doing?

Your thoughts:

_____

_____

_____

_____

You might say to her:

_____

_____

_____

_____

If she has little language, you might say to her:

_____

_____

_____

_____

What might this little girl be doing?

Our thoughts:

1. She is making a number of symmetrical buildings.
2. A few things she has made are not symmetrical, but the more we look at the picture, the more symmetrical constructions we see.
3. She seems to be trying out different block shapes to see their symmetrical properties.
4. She is also experimenting with balance, both physical and visual.
5. She is concentrating on her work.
6. She appears to be right-handed.

We would really be interested in what she would say about all her constructions. Do they represent something? For example, is the construction with a square at the bottom, two pillars next, a unit block next, and a triangle on top a person?

You might say to her:

"You have really been working hard. Look at all the things you have made. Would you like to tell me about any of them?"

"Did you notice that they are the same on both sides? When something is the same on both sides, we call it symmetrical. You have made a lot of symmetrical things. I wonder how you did that."

"You had to really use your eyes to see the symmetry in your constructions."

If she has little language, you might say:

"Look! You made this, and this, and this." (Point to them.)

"You worked hard."

(Pointing the parts.) "Square. Two pillars. Unit block. Triangle. That's a lot."

Pretending

In this period, the children's buildings begin to have a purpose. They are not just buildings. The children use the long blocks on edge to build walls for rooms. They make furniture for the rooms. They begin to talk about what they are building. They say they are making a house. The building looks like a house, and the children use it for dramatic play. In this dramatic play, they make up stories and play different parts. Now they can use prop boxes. They can use a *found materials* box of all kinds of things like dishes left from frozen meals and paper towel rolls. The box can have material scraps and useful things you and the students find. In this period, children tend to plan ahead and ask staff for things to use in the block center. It is in this period that writing materials really start to be used. The children may do a play and make tickets, programs, posters, exit signs, and so on. They continue to use their own types of writing, but it is usually easier to read. Now it is important to find a place for a construction to stay up for days at a time.

Start with these materials in the block corner.

Store the blocks on shelves marked with photos or tracings of each kind of unit block. (Refer to chapter 5 for a list of essential items that should be in the block corner in every developmental period.)

- A complete set of wooden unit blocks. See the "Number of Unit Blocks to Have" chart on page 130 to find out how many you should have. It is more important to have the number of blocks recommended than to have a wide variety of different kinds of blocks. When you have a large number of unit blocks, the children can really explore their possibilities.

- A set of cardboard blocks—about forty of them with a place to store them.

- Some hardwood hollow blocks, if you can afford them. They can be stored on the floor. They give children experience with working with really heavy and awkward materials.

- A *found materials* box with material scraps, plastic food containers of various kinds, cardboard pieces, cardboard tubes, and anything else that you and the children think of.

- A clear space where the children's buildings will be able to stay up.

Watch and Listen

Does the child

- begin to talk about what she is building?
- say what the building is for?
- make up stories and play different parts?
- use props in pretending? (The child may name her buildings before this stage. This may happen after she looks at the building and notices it looks like the one she names.)
- begin to make written signs and other things like tickets, dollars, menus, and so on?

What to Do

If the child is doing a number of the things in "Watch and Listen," you can

- sit quietly by the child. Watch what she is doing. Notice and record if she
  - acts out things in her life (for example, talks on a block walkie-talkie as she might have heard an adult use it).
  - pretends using objects (a block for a telephone or a baby bottle).
  - pretends without objects (stirs on the block stove she has made without any kind of pot).
  - pretends actions and situations (says things like, " 'Tend I'm the fireman and the house is on fire").
  - pretends a story or action for at least ten minutes.
  - pretends a story or action with at least one other child.
  - carries on a pretend conversation as she plays with other children.

  (The above list describes stages of dramatic play development that are useful for you to know.)
- add props that fit the themes the child is using in her play.
- help a child who is standing outside the group enter the play if she wants to. (Suggest a role she might play. Help her ask if the other children would like the role added to their play. Help her simply ask if she can play.)
- suggest the child make the props she needs or pretend to use them. Help her think through ways to make things. (Be sure to listen to her ideas and let her try them.)

What to Say

If the children are actively pretending, they don't need you to say anything. At this stage, you will be doing more listening than talking.

- If a child is pretending by himself, you might join his play. "It looks like you are cooking. Can I join you?" If the child agrees, he may tell you what he wants you to do. Do what he says and role-play, taking his lead. Say what seems natural for the situation.

- If the children are using copies of real objects in their play, you might pick up a unit block and pretend it is a portable phone. "Oh dear, I forgot to tell my son to put the casserole in the oven. I better call him. (Pantomime pushing in the numbers.) 'Hi, Rick. I forgot to tell you about the casserole. At 4:30 would you put it in the oven at 350°? Thanks, I really appreciate your help. Love ya! Mom.' "

- If several children are playing, and the play seems to be the same day after day, you may want to join the play and add some new ideas. "I notice that you have been going to Disney World every day. Would you like to add a side trip to the Kennedy Space Center? We could see the space shuttle go up. What do you think?" "Are you flying again today? Have you ever thought of the fun of taking a train? I wonder how you could build a train."

- You might introduce pretending objects with words. "This table needs to be wiped off." Pretend to go to the sink, turn on the water, and pantomime wetting a rag and wringing it out. Go over to the block table and pantomime wiping off the table. "My, that syrup from breakfast has made a mess on this table."

- You might introduce a construction project. "I notice you are making a hospital here. Would you like to make an ambulance? What do you suppose we would need to make an ambulance?" Make a list with the children and bring in the things they have asked for. You might also ask parents to contribute things for the ambulance. You might take the children to see an ambulance. Before you take the field trip, you and the children could list the things they want to know about an ambulance. They would then make sure they got those questions answered. They could use the answers to add to the ambulance construction. This activity can be turned into a dictated story with photos or pictures drawn by the children.

What to Add

As the children get used to what you have out, add some of the things you kept back and remove some of the things the children seem tired of.

- Think about what you see the children doing. What will help them develop further?

- Add to what you say when you add things. For example, if you see them playing in a pretend garage, ask if they would like the garage prop box. (A prop box is a box filled with things that fit a theme. A garage prop box might have mechanic's tools, several flashlights, a piece of hose similar to that used as an air hose for tires, rags, and so on.)

- Have a digital camera for taking pictures of the children's creations. Use the pictures in books or on walls of the center.

- Be sure the children have enough blocks to work with.

It is during this period in the children's development that the dramatic play area can become a part of the block area. The children may decide they need a car or bus for their travels, so they will build one out of blocks. Sometimes they will build walls to a house and move the furniture from dramatic play into it. This is why it is important for the dramatic play center to be next to the block center.

- You will want to add prop boxes.

- You may add large boxes that the children can turn into ambulances, bulldozers, buses, and more.

- Add masking tape, cardboard, and markers.

- Add new *found items* that you think fit what they are pretending.

- Encourage the children and their families to add things to the *found materials* box.

What Are Children Learning in the Pretending Period?

MATH		
What the Child Does	**A Sample Learning Standard**	**Notes**
Counts things to find out how many he has	•Understands number concepts, vocabulary, quantities, and written numerals in meaningful ways	The child counts for a purpose. He uses the result to support what he is doing. For example, Tim is playing in the restaurant the children have built. Bob asks for five hamburgers. Tim goes to the shelf and gets five unit blocks and gives them to Bob.
Explains to an adult why he has sorted a collection of animals into different block enclosures	•Explains why and how objects are organized	The child can see several different ways things are the same or different. For example, Isaac says, "I put all the big cows in that barn and the little ones next to them in that barn. I put all the people in the house."
Decides to sort things in very definite ways	•Sorts, categorizes, classifies, and orders objects by more than one attribute	The child's understanding of classifying according to detail reaches a fine point. For example, Cody and Cory get into an argument. Cody says, "That tractor isn't a Case. It's a John Deere. Look! It's green and yellow and the wheels are different."
Thinks about numbers as he interacts with other children	•Develops increased abilities to combine, separate, and name "how many" concrete objects	The child is thinking with numbers. He sees a practical use for numbers. For example, David counts to share blocks. "You can have three of mine." "I will give you five unit blocks for five of your pillars."

•Quoted from the Pennsylvania Early Learning Standards

What Are Children Learning in the Pretending Period?

TALKING AND LISTENING		
What the Child Does	**A Sample Learning Standard**	**Notes**
Answers questions adults ask willingly	•Accepts responsibility for learning through active participation, verbally or nonverbally	When the child is involved in making a block building, she answers questions adults ask, like, "How many units are you using to make that stove?"
Discusses her ideas with other children. Roles are given out and role-playing begins.	▲Participates in a variety of dramatic play activities that become more extended and complex	The standard is a social skills standard, but it is very useful for developing different kinds of speaking and listening skills in the child. She learns more and more language by talking with other children and with adults.

•Quoted from the Pennsylvania Early Learning Standards
▲Quoted from the Head Start Child Outcomes Framework

What might these children be doing?

Your thoughts:

_____

_____

_____

_____

You might say to them:

_____

_____

_____

_____

What might these children be doing?

Our thoughts:

1. They might be involved in a pretend play activity. (We would have to listen to them and watch them to be sure.)
2. They have constructed several piles of blocks.
3. Notice the boy who is bridging with a block.
4. They are all wearing hard hats. We wonder if this is a part of the play or a safety policy of the classroom.
5. Three of the kids seem to be involved in their play.

With all that is going on here, you will probably have a hard time talking to them about what they are doing. It would probably be better to watch and listen and record as much as you can. Later in the day, when they are quiet, tell them what you saw and heard. Ask them what they think about what you wrote. Is that what they were doing? Do they like the story? Would they like you to type it on the computer and make a book for them? Would they like to illustrate the book? At this stage, they might begin to be able to write a few words or even sentences themselves. Some could copy what you wrote.

You might say to them:

Here, you may really want to watch and listen before you say anything. You want to know what is happening before you comment. You might record what they are saying. Then read it back to them later in the day, saying,

> "This is the story I heard you playing in the blocks today."

> "Would you like me to make it into a book?"

> "Would you like to make pictures for it?"

What might this little girl be doing?

Your thoughts:

_____

_____

_____

_____

You might say to her:

_____

_____

_____

_____

If she has little language, you might say to her:

_____

_____

_____

_____

What might this little girl be doing?

Our thoughts:

1. She has created the inside of a house, making walls and using a *Gothic arch* for a doorway.
2. She has put in furniture and is putting a doll on a bed.
3. She is putting the doll in with her left hand. Is that because she has another doll in her other hand, or is she left-handed?
4. She seems to be concentrating on what she is doing.

You might say to her:

"It looks like a house."

"Would you like to tell me about it?"

"I wonder who is living in your house."

"Tell me about your family."

"I see a big bed in your house."

"I wonder who sleeps there."

"What other furniture do you need for your house?"

You would not ask all these questions at once. Use one or two as conversation starters.

If she has little language, you might say:

"Your house."

"You built it?"

"Who lives there?"

"Mom, Dad, Muffin (her dog), Beth?" (Be sure you know who's in her family.)

10

Making Known Things

This period is probably the most exciting of all. It is where everything that the children have been learning about blocks is used to perfection. The children tend to build miniatures of buildings they know about. They take field trips to draw and study their town. They return excited and start to build what they have studied. It becomes a miniature town with details. They make the buildings in the town recognizable. Frequently, each child will take responsibility for one building. They will use what they find to make tiny props. They might make food for the grocery store out of playdough. They might make books for a library. They may also start to ask questions about the way the city runs. Where does the electricity come from, for example? The children research to find out. Some of their villages will even have electric lights and elevators. In laying out the town, they will begin to develop mapping skills. They will measure all kinds of things. This sort of play helps skills improve naturally. It would be rare to see this period in children below kindergarten age. It can be seen in children all through elementary school.

Start with these materials in the block corner.

Store the blocks on shelves marked with photos or tracings of each kind of unit block. (Refer to chapter 5 for a list of essential items that should be in the block corner in every developmental period.) Names of the blocks should be printed in lowercase letters on the patterns or on the photos.

- A complete set of wooden unit blocks. See the "Number of Unit Blocks to Have" chart on page 130 to find out how many you should have. The more blocks you have, the better. They will encourage building in this period. When you have a large number of unit blocks, the children can really explore their possibilities.

- Move the large blocks out of the block center. They take up room and detract from the children's miniature building. If you still want them to encourage dramatic play, put them in the dramatic play area.

- Provide an organized area with all kinds of materials for making miniature things. Store them neatly in boxes—playdough, Popsicle sticks, shells, beads, thin wire, pipe cleaners, sequins, glue, and tape.

- Provide materials used in building miniature models, such as green-dyed moss.

- Provide bins of play people and vehicles.

Watch and Listen

Does the child

- talk about building a building the children know—a grocery store, the school, the firehouse?
- seem to know what he wants to build?
- want to label the construction?
- talk about what he needs for the building?
- use the finished construction for pretend play with others?
- work with others to create the building?
- build a complex building with lots of blocks?
- have lots of questions about how buildings are made and other things connected with what is being made?
- show interest in researching to find out more about what he wants to know?

What to Do

If the child is doing a number of the things in "Watch and Listen," you can

- sit or stand near where the child is working. Record what he is doing.
- respond to the child positively. Give him the supplies he asks for. If you don't have them, encourage him to think of substitutes.
- help the child take photos of the building he wants to build.
- allow the building to continue over several days. Encourage the child to write a sign that says something like, "Under construction. Don't break."
- allow the building to stay up as long as the child is playing with it. Encourage the child to write a sign that says, "In use. Don't take down."
- encourage the child to research in whatever media he can use.
- have group meetings to report on the project's progress. Ask questions and encourage the children to ask questions. Turn the questions into group projects.
- encourage the use of other materials to add to the building.
- encourage the making of miniature props.
- take the child on field trips to measure buildings, then draw them.

- encourage the child to get answers from people involved with the building.

- encourage the child to make written and illustrated project reports.

- bring in experts to talk about the project. Parents may have knowledge to share.

What to Say

If the children are actively constructing and/or pretending, you don't need to say anything. At this point, it is likely the children are so involved in the project, they would not want to answer questions.

At this stage, you will be doing more listening than talking. When you are sitting with the children at lunch, or in a group meeting, start a conversation about what you observed. Use questions like these to get the conversation going:

"I'm interested in your grocery store. How did you make those walls?"

"How did you make it so straight and square?"

"You were having trouble with the door. Tell me how you finally worked it out."

"You used almost all the classroom blocks to make your store. I wonder how many blocks are in each wall?"

"I wonder which wall is the longest?"

"Do you suppose the front wall is the same length as the back wall? Are they equal? How could we figure that out? I wonder if we could find architectural drawings of a grocery store on the Internet."

At another time, you might pose a problem with two groups of children. Give each group fifteen of the same kinds of blocks. See what each group builds. Have them look at each other's construction. Notice similarities and differences.

"Group one's building is tall and narrow. Group two's building is short and wide."

Label the two buildings for the rest of the class to see.

"Look at how group one used several units to make double units since they didn't have enough."

"Group two used the triangles for decorations."

Write a class story about each building. Encourage the children who are writing by this stage to write their own story.

What to Add

As the children get used to what you have out, add some of the things you kept back. Remove some of the things the children seem tired of.

- Think about what you see the children doing. What will help them develop further?

- Add to what you say when you add things. If you see them making a grocery store, offer them the playdough and suggest, "I thought you might like to make something for your grocery with this."

- Have a digital camera for taking pictures of the children's creations. Encourage the children to make their own pictures. Use them in books, reports, and charts on walls.

- Be sure the children have enough blocks to work with.

- Add paper, writing tools, masking tape, stapled booklets of blank paper, tongue depressors or Popsicle sticks, colored paper, and scissors.

- Add anything the children think of that they need (if you have it available).

- Encourage research, using the library and the Internet for picture or construction information.

- Provide measuring tools like tape measures, calipers, and yardsticks.

- Add tiny found items to the collection.

What Are Children Learning in the Making Known Things Period?

MATH		
What the Child Does	**A Sample Learning Standard**	**Notes**
Builds a block building from a picture in a book	•Recognizes geometric shapes in books, artwork, and the environment	The child can build block buildings from pictures. For example, Hailee creates a copy of the Empire State Building in blocks from pictures in books and on the Internet.
Talks about the basic features of shapes	▪Predicts how shapes can be changed by combining or dividing them	The child can understand parts of shapes like half circles. She can see how two like triangles make a square or rectangle. She understands how shapes are composed of angles, lines, and curves. She can analyze the composition of a shape. For example, Alexis points out to Maddison as she puts a half unit on a unit that a square is a rectangle, too, because it has four square angles and two sets of parallel lines.
Uses measuring tools to accurately measure a structure she wants to copy	•Uses standard and nonstandard measures in everyday situations	The child is comfortable with the concept of measurement and its practical purposes. For example, Nancy lays out the street of her little town. They make sure it is the same width from beginning to end. They use a ruler and measure.
Recognizes odd three-sided figures as triangles	▪Finds and describes geometric figures in real life	The child can use rules of geometry to name any figure that fits the rule. For example, Rosa explains to her teacher that a very flat triangle is a triangle because it has three corners and three sides.

•Quoted from the Pennsylvania Early Learning Standards
▪Quoted from the Pennsylvania Academic Standards

What Are Children Learning in the Making Known Things Period?

TALKING AND LISTENING

What the Child Does	A Sample Learning Standard	Notes
Takes part in group meetings about block building projects	▪Contributes to discussions. Asks relevant questions. Responds with appropriate information or opinions to questions asked. Listens to and acknowledges the contributions of others. Displays appropriate turn-taking behavior.	The child is able to use listening and speaking skills to work with others to create what he wants to build. For example, J.R. decides he wants to build a copy of the local grocery store with blocks. He works with some of his friends to plan what they will need and what it will look like.
Explains to adults a classroom project	▪Speaks using skills appropriate to formal speech situations	The child is able to speak effectively with adults because he has had opportunities for conversation during his preschool years. For example, Joshua is able to explain to adults who visit the classroom how the block hospital was planned and built.
Evaluates his work and that of others	▪Participates in small- and large-group discussions and presentations	The child has learned how to evaluate his own and others' creative work through conversations and discussions with the adults in the classroom. For example, Tony talks with his friends about what is good in the grocery store project and where it could be improved.

▪Quoted from the Pennsylvania Academic Standards

What might this little boy be doing?

Your thoughts:

_____

_____

_____

_____

You might say to him:

_____

_____

_____

_____

What might this little boy be doing?

Our thoughts:

1. This boy has decided to make the White House.
2. He has an internal picture of the columns and the circular elements and the side wings. He is aware of the building's symmetry.
3. He has not done any research to find a picture.
4. He is working from memory.
5. He appears to be definitely right-handed.
6. See how he is concentrating.
7. He needs to have a sign for his construction, perhaps because he is not comfortable that it is recognizable.

The teacher might want to ask him what he would like to know about the building, if he could research it. She might want to know what other materials or things he would like to have to add to the building. She might be interested in what he already knows about the building. Some teachers might end up giving him some kind of an assignment based on his construction and what he has said.

You might say to him:

"To me your building looks like the White House."

"I am really curious why you chose to make it."

"Are you interested in that period of architecture?"

"I really wonder what you would like to know about the White House."

"Have you studied it? What kinds of things do you know about it?"

"It is not easy to build a building like the White House."

"How did you think through the construction? Where did you start?"

What might this little girl be doing?

Your thoughts:

_____

_____

_____

_____

You might say to her:

_____

_____

_____

_____

What might this little girl be doing?

Our thoughts:

1. She has created a large house.
2. Notice how she is able to map the floor plan of her house. She even makes some rooms larger than other rooms.
3. She can build each room with a doorway in it.
4. She seems to be roofing over some of the rooms.
5. She appears to be right-handed.
6. She is concentrating on her work.

You might say to her:

"This looks like a house."

"Can you tell me about it?"

If she says it is her house, you might ask, "Can you show me your room?"

"Who lives in your house with you?"

"Can you show me the living room?"

"I am curious. Why have you put roofs on some of the rooms?"

"Would you like to dictate a story to me about your house?"

Safety

Safety is the most important thing to consider in every classroom. Blocks can be dangerous. The major danger in the block area tends to be human error. Sometimes this is because there are too many children in the available space. This may call for limiting the number of children who can work in the block area at one time. Throughout this book, we have noted that blocks require a lot of space. When you set up a room, plan the block space first. It should take up one-third of the room space during block playtime. You may make this possible by having some movable dividers or other ways to open the space up. When you have adequate space for blocks, there are fewer chances for the children to hurt each other with blocks by accident. Also, it is essential to have plenty of unit blocks. When there are plenty of blocks, you have fewer fights over them. With plenty of blocks, children also are better able to explore the possibilities of blocks. Still, you are likely to have a few special safety problems with blocks. The most common of these are addressed in this chapter.

Watch and Listen

Does the child throw or hit with blocks?

What to Do

If the child is younger than four, gently remove him from the area and explain privately that you cannot let him throw blocks because someone could get hurt. Tell him matter-of-factly that if he throws blocks again, he will need to play somewhere else for a while. Ask him if he would like to throw a ball or beanbag into a basket instead of playing with the blocks. Balls and beanbags are for throwing, blocks are not.

If the child is four, five, or older, he should be able to think through rules about this. Here is a process for helping children develop classroom rules:

1. Call the class together for a class meeting.

2. Describe the problem. ("Some people are hitting other people with blocks.")

3. Discuss what the dangers of this are and make a list on big paper.

4. Discuss the need for a rule to protect people.

5. Develop a rule. ("No one may hit anyone with blocks because it hurts.")

6. Develop a consequence. This is important, because a rule without a consequence has no power. If the children determine the consequence, it has more meaning for them. ("If someone hits with a block, that person must stay out of the block area for a day.")

7. Write the rule on a big piece of paper. Ask someone to illustrate or decorate it, and then post it where it will be remembered and have meaning for the children.

Children obey best the rules and consequences they have developed themselves. Sometimes you may develop a general rule with the children for a problem like hitting instead of a specific one for the block center. For a general rule, you will have to make a generally agreed-upon consequence.

Watch and Listen

Does the child build high towers?

What to Do

Children who are able to build high towers should be able to develop rules about them. Develop rules with the children as in the earlier example. Some possible rules might be:

1. Always wear hard hats in the block area.

2. Have a teacher there when you want to build a really tall tower.

3. Have only two children and a teacher in the block area when building a high tower.

4. Limit the height of the tower to the children's shoulder height. (This rule limits the possibilities of the blocks, but safety is so important that you might think it is worth it. An alternative is to find short three-step stepladders and teach children how to use them safely so that they can build higher.)

5. Use only smaller blocks—like cube-shaped alphabet blocks—to build high towers.

6. Build the tower against a wall so it has support.

Don't forget that when you develop a rule, you need a consequence, too.

Watch and Listen

Does the child take blocks from others?

What to Do

Help the child to understand that someone else was using that block. Talk with her about not taking blocks that other people are using. Tell her she can ask the other person for the block, but she can't take it. Be sure that she understands the difference. Help her to know that if she wants a block and someone doesn't want to give it to her, she should come to you. You will help her solve her problem.

When she comes to you, take the child on your lap and talk with her about the problem. Tell her you understand that she wants that block. Say, "You really want that block, don't you? I wish you could have it, too. Right now, Josey is using it. When she finishes, you can have it. Would you like to sit here with me for a while? Could we find another block like it for you? Let's see if we can find something else for you to play with." Then take her to try to find something. Don't abandon her with "Go find something else to play with."

Always listen to the child's feelings and comfort her. Always say that you understand how much she wants the thing. Help her to understand that you wish she could have it. Help her also to understand that sometimes adults can't give people things, no matter how much they wish they could.

When you listen to children's feelings and tell them what you have heard, they are comforted. They are then able to cope with disappointment. Someone understands and cares about their feelings. Giving them words for their feelings is another way to give them power. Say something like, "I know you are so disappointed. You really want that block" or "I see you are frustrated. You really wanted to finish your tower, and there aren't enough units." This helps children understand that there is a word for what they are feeling and gives them words to use another time. If you tell them to stop crying or that they are being silly, they still have the unhappy feeling and may need to get it out by doing something you don't want them to do.

When you work with the children, make a point of sharing blocks with them. At a class meeting, use puppets to show a story of a puppet who doesn't share and what happens to it. Then show the story of a puppet who does share and what happens to it. Talk about the two stories with the children.

Watch and Listen

Does the child knock down other children's blocks?

What to Do

This may not be intentional. Often, children knock down block towers by mistake. It would help to ask the children involved to tell in their own words what happened. Help them to listen to each other. After the explanation, decide with the children what the problem is. It may be that there is a need for people to be more careful where they walk. They may need to handle the long blocks more carefully. They may need to think about where the end of the long block is going. Use this problem-solving technique with them:

1. Decide what the problem is.

2. Brainstorm solutions. (When you brainstorm, you list all solutions suggested. It doesn't matter how silly or crazy they may be. No idea is put down or made fun of.)

3. Go through the list of ideas. Cross off those that everyone agrees won't work. Choose from the list the ones everyone thinks are worth trying. Decide on one to try.

4. Plan how to put the solution in action.

5. Try the solution.

6. Evaluate how it worked. Did it solve the problem? If it didn't, why? Would you want to modify it and try it again? Do you want to go back to the list and find another solution to try? Then go through steps 4, 5, and 6 again.

If some children are knocking down others' buildings on purpose, then the problem may need to be talked about by the class. Use a puppet story as suggested on page 122 to help discuss the problem. You may want to try the problem-solving technique shown above with the class, too. You may need to develop a rule.

Our Own Problems

This page is for you to record problems that your classroom has had with blocks other than those given here. Record the problem and then add the solutions you found that worked.

Useful Information

Help with Cleanup

Store the blocks neatly on shelves. Draw around the most recognizable side of the blocks to make a pattern. Put block-shape patterns on the shelves by painting them on or cutting them out of adhesive-backed or laminated paper, then sticking them on the shelves. Put the block names on the shapes. An adult should help the children clean up the blocks in the beginning. The adult can help them sort and match each block to its shape. This will teach sorting, classifying, and organizing. These are math skills. The children will gradually learn to shelve blocks by themselves. We have seen classrooms where a group of children cleaned up the whole block area by themselves while the teacher went on with an activity with the rest of the class. When they can do this, they are very proud of their ability. This is very good for a healthy self-esteem.

Please remember that cleanup time is one of your most important chances to teach! It is not a time of unpleasant work, but a great time for teaching and learning. Value and love cleanup time!

Photos

Take photos of the children's block structures. Post the photos on the wall or in an album. The children will love looking at them. This helps to develop self-esteem. It also helps children learn to talk about the past. Seeing the photos may also encourage the children to talk about what they are going to build with the blocks. This is talking about the future and planning. These are language and thinking skills. If you take a sequence of photos and laminate them, the children can practice putting the photos in order. This will help them learn sequencing—another math skill. Take photos of the structures from different perspectives: from above, from the side, from the front, and so on. This will give the children experience with point of view. In the later developmental periods, the children should be able to use a digital camera to make their own pictures.

Care of Blocks

For many years, unit blocks have been made of hard wood. Be sure to buy the hard maple blocks. They are worth the money as they can last almost forever without a great deal of care. They are usually unfinished. Keep them covered when not in use to keep them as clean as possible. If they get dirty, you can wash them. Don't soak them in water, however, as it might cause them to crack. When you clean them, work quickly with a stiff brush, using dishwashing detergent and water. Then wipe off any extra moisture and let them air dry thoroughly before they are played with again. Children can help with some of the washing and drying steps. They can also sand and wax the blocks, as described in the next paragraph, if you are comfortable with them doing it.

After a number of years, if you notice that the blocks are beginning to splinter, sand the splintery edges with a fine sandpaper, trying not to destroy the bevels on the edges of the blocks. You can put a wood-paste wax finish on them after sanding. Goddard's Cabinet Maker's Wax is a good wax to use. Don't oil them with linseed or other oils, however, as oils do not dry and they tend to collect dirt.

If you need to disinfect your blocks, wipe them with a damp rag. Use a solution of one-quarter cup household bleach mixed into one gallon of water. Mix this cleaning solution fresh every day. Rinse the blocks with clean tap water after disinfecting them. Dry them as recommended above.

In recent years, programs have had the choice of buying foam unit blocks. They are the same sizes and shapes as the wooden unit blocks. They usually come in red, blue, green, and yellow. Before you buy whole sets, try them out. They have entirely different qualities than wooden blocks. They are lighter. They stick to each other. They do not slide. They do not build as high. They squash and bend. This affects their stability. They smell different. Children tend to bite them and leave marks. In other words, they provide a very different experience for the children. In many classrooms, they are mixed with wooden blocks. This tends to confuse the children's study of blocks. They have to begin to recognize that one kind of double unit does things one way, and another does them another way.

Foam blocks are frequently bought because people are afraid of the wooden blocks. They fear the children will hurt each other with the wooden blocks. This certainly is a danger; however, the suggestions for safety in this book as well as the suggestions in each of the chapters should help prevent children from being injured by blocks. For countless years, children have used and learned from wooden unit blocks. They provide their own special experience. We would hate to see children lose this important chance.

Number of Unit Blocks to Have

Unit blocks are wooden blocks based on a "unit" block that measures $1^3/_8$ x $2^3/_4$ x $5^1/_2$ inches. Truthfully, there is no ideal number of blocks to have. You will probably find that you never have enough. Every list of suggested blocks is different. Usually, you will find that any list will suggest more blocks than you have. This is our list.

Block Name	Two Years	Three Years	Four Years	Five Years
Half unit	24	48	48	60
Unit	24	180	192	220
Double unit	0	96	140	190
Quadruple unit	0	48	48	72
Pillar	24	24	48	72
Half pillar	0	0	12	16
Half column	10	20	32	40
Column	0	12	16	20
Circle curve	0	8	16	20
Half circle curve and quarter circle	0	12	16	20
Ramp	0	12	32	40
Roman arch and small half circle	0	0	3	6
Crossroad	0	0	4	8
Gothic arch and Gothic door	0	2	2	4
Half Gothic arch and small buttress	0	0	0	4
Side road	0	0	2	4
Floor board	0	12	32	40
Roof board	0	0	12	20
Right angle	0	0	2	4
Large triangle	0	8	16	24
Small triangle	16	8	16	18

Some catalogs may list other kinds of blocks or use different block names than are on this list. Try to establish a uniform set of names within your program. Use the names used by the company that you bought the blocks from.

Photos of Unit Blocks

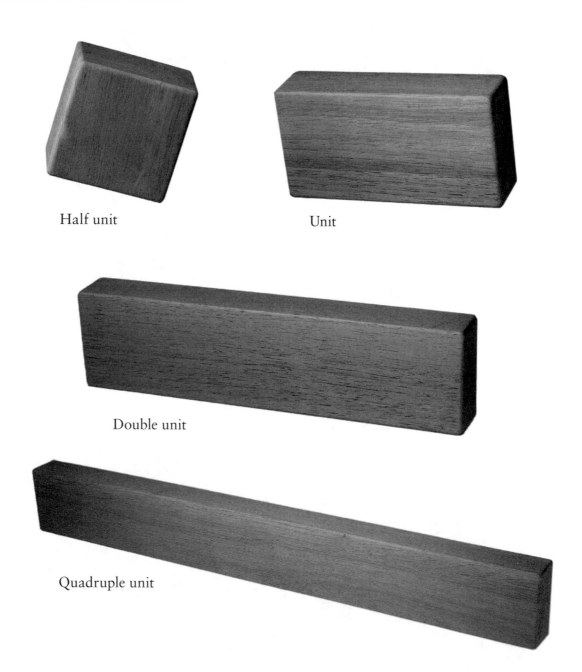

Half unit

Unit

Double unit

Quadruple unit

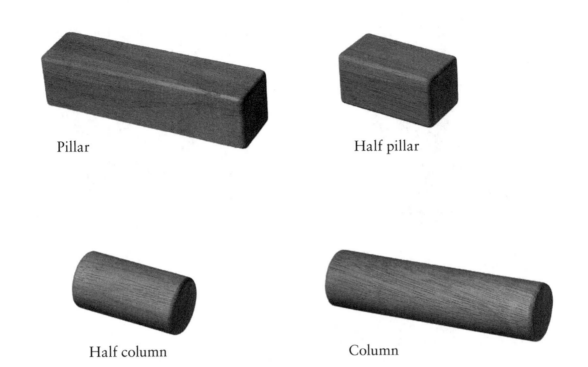

Pillar

Half pillar

Half column

Column

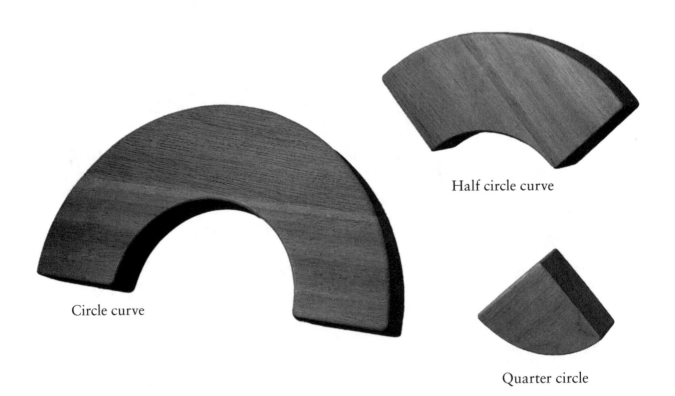

Half circle curve

Circle curve

Quarter circle

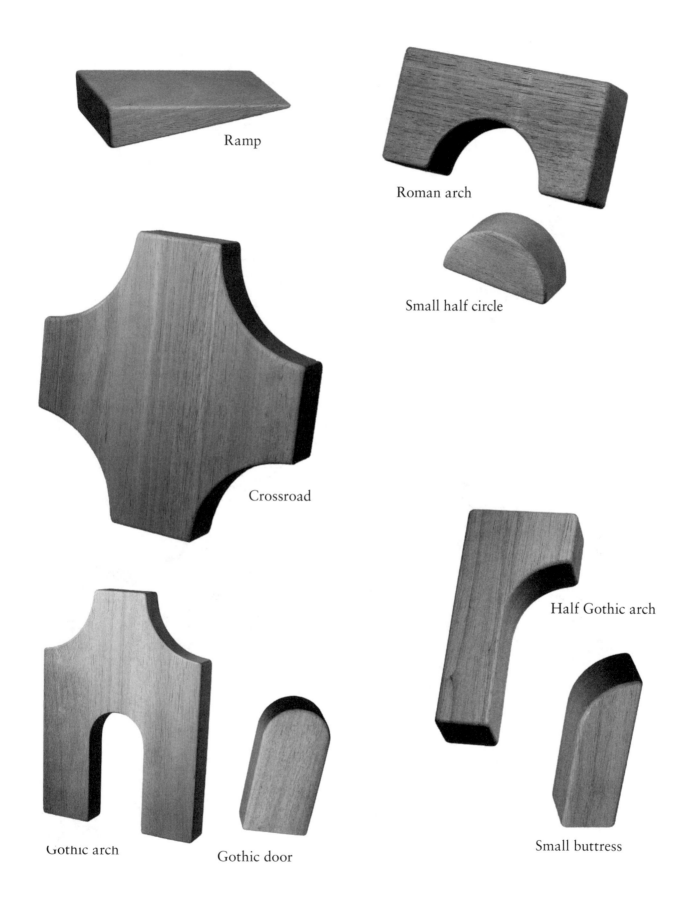

Ramp

Roman arch

Small half circle

Crossroad

Gothic arch

Gothic door

Half Gothic arch

Small buttress

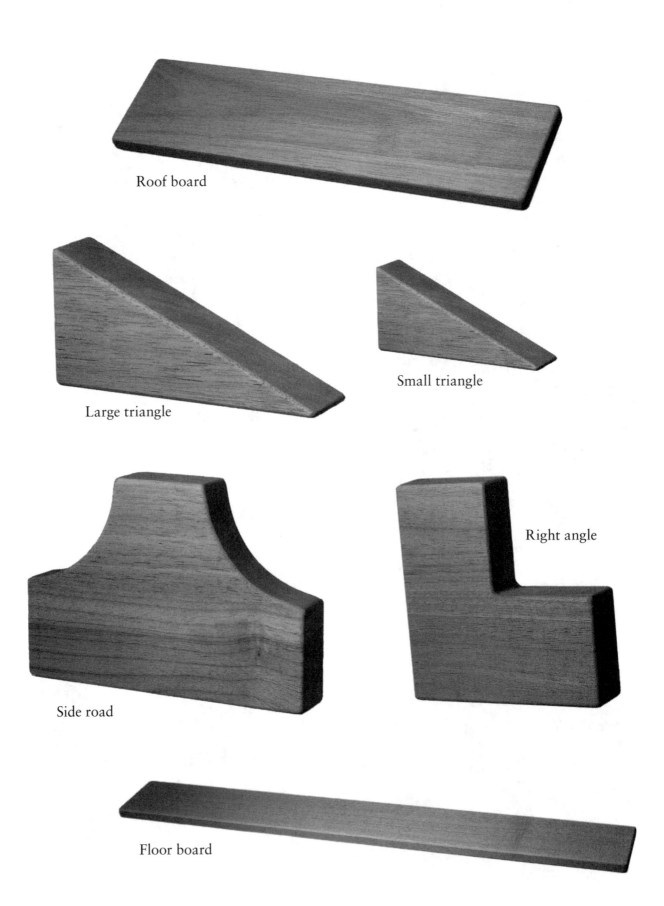

Roof board

Large triangle

Small triangle

Side road

Right angle

Floor board

Useful Reading

Chalufour, Ingrid, and Karen Worth. *Building Structures with Young Children*. St. Paul, MN: Redleaf Press, 2004.

> This is a set of materials from Redleaf's Young Scientist series. It includes a teacher's guide, a trainer's guide, and a video. This is an exciting, full course that might be considered an extension of this book. It teaches thorough studies of structures with children using appropriate inquiry-based techniques. The video gives excellent examples of teachers interacting with children.

Church, Ellen Booth, et al. *Learning through Play: Blocks*. New York: Scholastic, 1990.

> This is a useful, easy-to-read book about blocks. It talks about the value of block play, block play development, and the teacher's role in block play, and it provides a number of block play activities for different ages from two to five years. The ideas are mostly activities directed by adults. The best way for children to learn about blocks is for them to have enough blocks, space, and time to explore them in their own developmental way.

Dodge, Diane Trister. *The Creative Curriculum for Early Childhood*, 3rd ed. Washington, DC: Teaching Strategies, 1993.

> This book has a chapter that provides a thorough discussion of the practical aspects of the block center and its use.

Hirsch, Elisabeth S., ed. *The Block Book*, rev. ed. Washington, DC: National Association for the Education of Young Children, 1996.

> This is the best existing book about blocks. It discusses the stages of block play development in detail. It describes with examples what children actually do. It also covers block building as an art and as a way to learn science, math, and social studies. It has a chapter on blocks and dramatic play. Appendixes include suggested equipment for block building. Photographs and drawings illustrate the stages of block play development.

Other Resources from Redleaf Press

Building Structures with Young Children

Ingrid Chalufour & Karen Worth, Education Development Center, Inc.

 Building Structures with Young Children guides children's explorations to help deepen their understanding of the physical science present in building block structures—including concepts such as gravity, stability, and balance.

#409301-BR   **$25.95**

More Than Letters: Literacy Activities for Preschool, Kindergarten, and First Grade

Sally Moomaw, MEd, & Brenda Hieronymus

 More Than Letters contains dozens of fun and engaging ideas for nurturing reading and writing skills. Chapters explore how the use of big books, interactive charts, games, and manipulative materials can fill a classroom with meaningful print.

#300301-BR   **$24.95**

More Than Counting: Whole Math Activities for Preschool and Kindergarten

Sally Moomaw, MEd, & Brenda Hieronymus

 More Than Math includes more than 100 ideas for unusual new manipulatives, collections, grid games, path games, graphing, and gross-motor play that combine to make a complete math experience for children.

#301901-BR   **$25.95**

Weaving the Literacy Web: Creating Curriculum Based on Books Children Love

Hope Vestergaard

 Using books as the centerpiece for fun, *Weaving the Literacy Web* provides a framework for developing engaging, developmentally appropriate curriculum in the preschool classroom.

#316401-BR   **$19.95**

Make Early Learning Standards Come Alive: Connecting Your Practice and Curriculum to State Guidelines

Gaye Gronlund, MA

 Clear explanations of how to make early learning standards come alive in classrooms and programs are provided in this practical and supportive resource. Easy-to-read charts show how different states define standards and how these standards can be addressed in the classroom.

#536401-BR   **$24.95**

Use Your Words: How Teacher Talk Helps Children Learn

Carol Garhart Mooney

 The connection between the ways we speak and the ways children behave and learn are examined in this humorous and thoughtful guide. Commonly missed opportunities to support cognitive development through meaningful conversation, develop receptive language and expressive language, and avoid and address behavioral issues in the classroom are looked at closely.

#155401-BR   **$18.95**

Product availability and pricing are subject to change without notice.

800-423-8309 • www.redleafpress.org